D0793754

THE
Special Educational Needs
Co-ordinator's
HANDBOOK

A Guide for Implementing
the Code of Practice

GARRY HORNBY
GREGAN DAVIS
and
GEOFF TAYLOR

NATIONAL UNIVERSITY
LIBRARY FRESNO

London and New York

First published 1995
by Routledge
11 New Fetter Lane, London EC4P 4EE

Simultaneously published in the USA and Canada
by Routledge
29 West 35th Street, New York, NY 10001

© 1995 Garry Hornby, Gregan Davis and Geoff Taylor

Typeset in Sabon by Solidus (Bristol) Limited

Printed in Great Britain by TJ Press Ltd, Padstow, Cornwall

All rights reserved. No part of this book may be reprinted or
reproduced or utilised in any form or by any electronic,
mechanical, or other means, now known or hereafter
invented, including photocopying and recording, or in any
information storage or retrieval system, without permission in
writing from the publishers.

British Library Cataloguing in Publication Data
A catalogue record for this book is available from the British Library

Library of Congress Cataloging in Publication Data
A catalogue record for this book has been requested

ISBN 0–415–11683–X

Contents

Figures

Acknowledgements

The authors would like to thank the following people for their help and advice at various stages of the project: Roger Kidd, Sue Faull, Selina Khoo and Marcia Pilgrim.

Thanks are also due to our editor, Helen Fairlie, for her support, encouragement and efficiency throughout the publication process.

CHAPTER ONE

Meeting Special Educational Needs in Mainstream Schools

INTRODUCTION

The *Code of Practice on the Identification and Assessment of Special Educational Needs* (DfE, 1994) provides the most far reaching guidance on this subject ever aimed at teachers in mainstream schools. The Code presents regulations and guidance for the implementation of the sections of the 1993 Education Act which pertain to special educational needs generally and therefore will affect the whole field of special education. But it is with special educational provision in mainstream primary and secondary schools where its impact will be the greatest. Therefore, this is the major focus of the handbook.

The Code uses the estimate made in the Warnock Report (DES, 1978) that approximately 20 per cent of children in the UK will have special educational needs (SEN) at some stage of their school careers. It suggests that around 2 per cent of these will have SEN of a severity or complexity that Local Education Authorities (LEAs) will be required to arrange special educational provision by means of a statement of SEN. The remaining 18 per cent are expected to have their SEN met by their schools, with the help of outside specialists when necessary, but without the need for statements of SEN.

Where the Code differs from the guidance that accompanied the 1981 Education Act is that it places much more emphasis on meeting the needs of the 18 per cent of children with SEN in mainstream schools. The requirements of the Code place substantially increased demands on teachers in mainsteam schools, particularly SEN co-ordinators whose responsibilities are extensively detailed in the Code. The purpose of this book is therefore to help SEN co-ordinators and other teachers in mainstream schools to address the demanding task of implementing the Code.

DEFINITIONS

The definitions of special educational needs, special educational provisions and learning difficulties in the Code are the same as that used in the 1981 Education Act:

- *Special educational needs* are deemed to exist *if children have learning difficulties which require that special educational provision be made for them.*
- *Special educational provision* is defined as *educational provision which is over and above that generally made for children in mainstream schools.*
- *Learning difficulties* are deemed to exist if children have *significantly greater difficulty in learning than the majority of children of their age,* or, *if they have a disability that either prevents or hinders them from making use of the educational facilities generally available to their age peers.*

EVOLUTION OF MAINSTREAM PROVISION FOR MEETING SEN

The Code of Practice embodies the assumption that all teachers in mainstream schools are effectively teachers of children with SEN. This was not considered to be the case until relatively recently, as a brief summary of the evolution of mainstream provisions for children with SEN will demonstrate.

The first provisions for children with SEN in Britain were special schools for the blind and deaf which were first opened in the late eighteenth century and continued to be established throughout the nineteenth century (Cole, 1989; Hurt, 1988). Some institutions for children with physical disabilities were opened towards the end of the nineteenth century but provisions for those with learning difficulties were extremely limited until this time. It was the establishment of universal education through the passing of Education Acts in the 1870s and 1880s which focused attention on children with learning difficulties. Awareness grew that a substantial minority of children in ordinary schools had difficulties in learning which hindered the education of other children and led to unacceptable levels of school failure (Hegarty, 1993). There was pressure from teachers to create separate provision for such pupils, which led to the establishment of a gradually increasing number of special schools and special classes during the first half of this century. This trend was given further impetus by the publication of the 1944 Education Act.

The 1944 Education Act obliged LEAs to make provision for various categories of children with disabilities: blind; partially sighted; deaf; partially deaf; delicate; educationally subnormal; epileptic; physically handicapped;

and those with speech defects. The Act required LEAs to ascertain the needs of children for special educational treatment and recommended that they should be educated in ordinary schools wherever possible. However, in the years following the 1944 Act, a substantial proportion of children in the above categories were placed in special schools or special classes.

In the 1950s and 1960s numerous studies were conducted in the USA to evaluate the effectiveness of special classes. Despite the fact that the overall result of this research was equivocal, increasingly negative views about special classes and special schools developed amongst professionals in the field of education (Hornby, 1992). Legislation which emerged in the USA in 1974 and in the UK in 1976 encouraged the integration of children with SEN into mainstream schools but did not mandate it. The Warnock Report (DES, 1978) simply re-affirmed the intentions of the 1976 Education Act. Therefore, the 1981 Education Act, which was based on the Warnock Report, stated that children with SEN should be educated in mainstream schools as long as:

- this was in accordance with their parents' wishes;
- the child's SEN could be met in the mainstream school;
- the education of other children in the school would not suffer; and
- the placement was compatible with the efficient use of resources.

The 1988 Education Act affirmed this aspect of the 1981 Act and stipulated that all pupils with SEN should follow the National Curriculum to the maximum extent possible. The 1993 Education Act with its emphasis on the 18 per cent of pupils with SEN in mainstream schools has again affirmed the notion that the majority of children with SEN are to be educated in mainstream schools.

CURRENT PROVISIONS FOR MEETING SEN

The Code of Practice states that a continuum of special educational provision is needed in order to cater for the continuum of special educational needs which exist in schools (DfE, 1994, p. 2). Actual SEN provision in the UK currently ranges from placement in a mainstream classroom with no additional help through to placement in a residential special school (Leadbetter and Leadbetter, 1993). A typical continuum of SEN provision available in most LEAs is illustrated below.

1 *Mainstream classroom with differentiated work.* Children with SEN are catered for by classroom teachers providing differentiated curriculum

material. That is, activities are planned in such a way that they can be completed at different levels or in different ways depending on children's abilities. For example, when teaching mathematics, a number of easier items can be provided for pupils with mild learning difficulties and several more difficult items can be included in order to challenge pupils who may be gifted in this subject.

2 *Mainstream classroom with small group teaching.* Children with SEN are taught by their teacher in the mainstream classroom but for part or possibly all of the time receive their tuition in a small group of pupils or on a one-to-one basis. For example, the class teacher provides additional tuition to a group of three or four children with reading difficulties while the rest of the class get on with their work.

3 *Mainstream classroom with support teaching.* Children with SEN receive all their tuition in mainstream classes but are supported in some subject areas by an additional teacher who comes into the class. Support teaching may be carried out by the SEN co-ordinator or other staff with a major responsibility for SEN. However, in some schools support teaching in each subject area is conducted by other teachers from the same department or faculty. Some pupils, such as those with moderate learning difficulties, may be supported across the curriculum whereas others, such as those with specific learning difficulties, may only be supported in their weak subject(s).

4 *Mainstream classroom with withdrawal.* Children with SEN receive most of their tuition in mainstream classrooms but are withdrawn to a resource room for some subjects in order to receive tuition, typically in basic literacy or numeracy skills, from the SEN co-ordinator or other school staff with major responsibility for SEN. For example, pupils with difficulties in reading and writing may be withdrawn to the SEN department, or a resource room, for individual or small group tuition during their English lessons.

5 *Mainstream classroom with assistance from outside specialist.* Children with SEN are taught in mainstream classes with the assistance of an outside specialist such as a peripatetic learning support teacher, member of the hearing impaired service, or speech therapist. The specialist may work directly with a child in the classroom, in another room in the school, or have the child attend their clinic outside the school. Alternatively, or in addition, the specialist may provide guidance to the class teacher regarding the child's SEN. For example, a pupil with specific learning difficulties may have tuition from a peripatetic teacher for one lesson per week and for the remainder of the week work on a programme designed by the peripatetic teacher which is supervised by the class teacher.

6 *Unit in a mainstream school with time in mainstream classroom.*

Children with SEN receive most of their tuition in a unit or resource room within the mainstream school but attend mainstream classes in some subjects and are integrated socially for such things as school assemblies and playtimes. Pupils are typically integrated into mainstream classes for the subjects which are their particular strengths. For example, one pupil may be integrated for physical education, another for geography.

7 *Unit in mainstream school*. Children with SEN receive all their tuition in a classroom or separate unit within the mainstream school but are integrated socially for such things as school assemblies and playtimes.

8 *Special school with mainstream links*. Children with SEN receive most of their tuition in a special school but attend a mainstream school for possibly half a day or a whole day per week. Such links provide special school pupils with opportunities for social integration with children in mainstream schools.

9 *Special school full-time*. Children with SEN receive all their tuition at a special school. Currently, in the UK, most non-residential special schools cater for children with either moderate learning difficulties, severe learning difficulties or physical disabilities.

10 *Residential special school with day attendance*. Children with SEN attend the residential special school during the day but return home each night and for weekends.

11 *Residential special school full-time*. Children with SEN receive all their tuition and live during term time at a residential special school. Currently in the UK most residential special schools cater for children with emotional and behavioural problems or severe sensory impairments such as those who are blind, deaf or deaf-blind.

TYPES OF SEN

The Code of Practice refers to eight different types of special educational need: learning difficulties; specific learning difficulties; emotional and behavioural difficulties; physical disabilities; hearing difficulties; visual difficulties; speech and language difficulties; and medical conditions. These are described briefly below. Further details can be found in books which provide an overview of the various types of special educational needs (e.g. Gulliford and Upton,1992; Hallahan and Kauffman, 1991). Also described below is a ninth type of special need, termed 'gifted underachievement', which is not specifically included in the Code but which is implicit in the Code's principles and procedures and is likely to become of increasing interest to schools as the Code is implemented.

Learning difficulties

Children with learning difficulties make up the largest group of children with SEN. Learning difficulties range from *mild*, through *moderate* and *severe*, to *profound* and *multiple* learning difficulties. Children with severe, profound and multiple learning difficulties are small in number compared with those who have mild or moderate learning difficulties who make up the majority of this group. Children are identified as having *mild learning difficulties* if they are experiencing problems in acquiring basic literacy and numeracy skills. Children with *moderate learning difficulties* are, in addition, likely to have delayed speech and language development, poor social skills and also may exhibit emotional or behavioural difficulties. Children with *severe learning difficulties* are likely to have substantial problems in all these areas as well as possible problems in learning basic self-help skills such as dressing and toileting. Children with *profound* or *multiple learning difficulties* will have major problems in acquiring all of the above skills.

The vast majority of children with mild learning difficulties are found in mainstream classes. In the past, a large proportion of children with moderate learning difficulties were placed in special schools but increasingly these pupils are being educated in mainstream schools in either special units or mainstream classrooms. The majority of children with severe learning difficulties and those with profound or multiple learning difficulties are placed in special schools. However, many special schools have links with mainstream schools which enable an increasing number of these children to spend some of their time in ordinary schools.

Specific learning difficulties

Children with *specific learning difficulties* have problems in acquiring basic reading, writing, spelling or number skills despite having at least average levels of intellectual ability. There is usually a marked difference between their performance orally and on paper. The frustration generated by this situation can lead to such children exhibiting emotional or behavioural difficulties. The vast majority of children with specific learning difficulties are found in mainstream classrooms.

Emotional and behavioural difficulties

Children with *emotional or behavioural difficulties* exhibit behaviours which make it difficult for them to function effectively at school or disrupt the education of other pupils. For example, children may be withdrawn or depressed or display obsessions or phobias. Alternatively, they may exhibit anti-social or unco-operative behaviour. In many cases such pupils also experience significant difficulties in acquiring basic literacy and numeracy skills. A minority of children with emotional or behavioural problems attend residential special schools but the majority are in mainstream classrooms.

Physical disabilities

Children with *physical disabilities* make up one of the smaller groups of pupils with SEN. They include those whose disability has resulted from a congenital condition and others who have suffered an injury. Some physically disabled children, such as those with cerebral palsy or spina bifida, may also experience sensory and neurological impairments with consequent learning difficulties. Other children, whose physical disabilities have resulted from serious illnesses such as muscular dystrophy or cystic fibrosis, may experience emotional difficulties. Children who have an intellectual disability (such as severe learning difficulty) in addition to a physical disability are typically placed in special schools. However, the majority of children who have only a physical disability are educated in mainstream schools.

Hearing difficulties

Children with *hearing difficulties* make up probably the second largest group of children with SEN, after those with learning difficulties. Levels of hearing impairment range from mild and moderate to severe and profound. Children with mild or moderate losses are the most numerous and are typically placed in mainstream classes. Those with severe and profound losses tend to be placed in units in mainstream schools or in special schools. Children with all levels of hearing difficulties are at risk of experiencing problems in learning basic literacy and numeracy skills and may become withdrawn or disruptive in school.

Visual difficulties

Children with *visual difficulties* make up the smallest group of children with SEN. There is a wide range of levels of visual difficulty and also several differing forms of visul impairment each with different implications for the child's education. A small proportion of this group are totally blind and are mostly educated in special schools or units within ordinary schools. However, the vast majority of children with visual difficulties have what is termed partial sight or low vision and are found in mainstream classes or special units within mainstream schools.

Speech and language difficulties

Speech and language difficulties often co-exist with other disabilities, especially hearing impairment, cerebral palsy and moderate to profound levels of learning difficulties. Thus, the majority of children with more severe degrees of speech and language difficulties are found in special schools or units in mainstream schools. However, mild to moderate levels of such difficulties are common in mainstream classes. There are four types of difficulties: articulation problems (e.g. substituting r for w in speech); fluency problems (e.g. stutter); voice problems (e.g. hoarseness); and delayed receptive or expressive language.

Medical conditions

Children with *medical conditions* may have associated SEN for several reasons. Children with conditions such as epilepsy or asthma may require drug treatment which impairs their concentration. Children with life-threatening conditions such as heart disease, cancer, brain tumours or cystic fibrosis may need frequent hospital treatment which necessitates considerable absences from school. Other chronic conditions such as diabetes, eczema and rheumatoid arthritis may deplete a child's reserves of energy. Thus, all these medical conditions can have a negative impact on children's academic attainment. In addition the psychological impact of such conditions can lead to children experiencing emotional or behavioural difficulties.

Gifted underachievers

Although not mentioned in the Code of Practice because they are not generally included within the scope of special education, there is a group of children who can be considered to have special needs and would gain substantial benefit from the application of the procedures proposed by the Code. *Gifted underachievers* are children who may be performing at average levels in school subjects but whose learning potential is well above the average, suggesting that their academic achievements are not commensurate with their ability. For example, a child with above average intellectual ability who is performing academically at an average level in National Curriculum core subjects is underachieving. These pupils are likely to come to light in increasing numbers as schools implement the requirements of the Code such as school-wide screening of basic academic skills and learning potential and as information becomes available from National Curriculum assessments. Schools will find the procedures embodied in the Code, such as careful planning and monitoring of progress, to be useful in providing an optimum education for pupils who are gifted but are underachieving, in the same way that these procedures are useful for pupils traditionally considered to have

SEN. This is important in times when schools are looking to raise the standards achieved by all of their pupils. By including gifted underachievers within their brief SEN co-ordinators will be extending their role to contribute to the school in a broader context which will generally be much appreciated by the senior management and other teachers.

IMPLEMENTING THE CODE OF PRACTICE IN MAINSTREAM SCHOOLS

This handbook is mainly concerned with the implications of the Code for mainstream schools and therefore with children with SEN who are receiving their education in any of the options from 1 to 7 of the continuum of SEN provision described earlier in this chapter. One of the major concerns about the Code, which has been expressed by teachers responsible for pupils with SEN, is that the Government has made it clear that any changes which it requires are to be brought about without any additional money or resources being provided to schools or LEAs. It has been suggested that the existing resources which schools are given to cater for pupils with SEN should be sufficient for them to meet the requirements of the Code. Further, it is expected that resources from Grants for Education, Support and Training (GEST) will be diverted to fund the training needed by SEN co-ordinators, mainstream class teachers and governors to equip them for their responsibilities as set out in the Code. In this situation SEN co-ordinators are going to need guidance in order to design highly time-efficient procedures for operating the Code within schools as well as material which they can use for in-service training with their colleagues on the requirements of the Code. This handbook seeks to provide SEN co-ordinators with the guidance and training materials they will need. An overview of the contents of the handbook is presented below.

AN OVERVIEW OF THE HANDBOOK

Chapter One has provided a rationale for the handbook and discussed some issues which provide a background to the introduction of the Code. These were:

- the definitions of SEN, SEN provisions and learning difficulties used in the Code;
- the evolution of mainstream school provision for SEN;
- the continuum of provisions for meeting SEN;
- the various types of SEN likely to be encountered in mainstream schools.

Chapter Two provides an overview of the principles and procedures embodied in the Code and focuses on:

- the development of a comprehensive SEN policy and effective procedures for meeting SEN;
- the increased responsibilities for schools with regard to provisions for pupils with SEN;
- the importance of the role of SEN co-ordinators, class teachers and school governors;
- an overview of the 5-stage model for meeting SEN proposed in the Code.

Chapter Three focuses on meeting SEN from within the school's resources, that is stages 1 and 2 of the 5-stage model proposed in the Code. It includes:

- the roles and responsibilities of staff, especially the SEN co-ordinator;
- the collection of information from parents, pupils, the school and other sources;
- procedures for the identification and assessment of SEN and provisions for meeting SEN;
- the design of Individual Educational Plans (IEPs);
- arrangements for reviewing progress.

Chapter Four focuses on stage 3 of the 5-stage model which involves the school organising provision for children with SEN with the assistance of outside specialists. It includes:

- the role of the SEN co-ordinator in working with teachers, parents and specialists;
- designing and reviewing Individual Educational Plans (IEPs);
- the background and role of outside specialists who work with children with SEN;
- strategies for making the most effective use of outside specialists.

Chapter Five focuses on the SEN co-ordinator's responsibilities in the assessment and statementing procedures at stages 4 and 5 of the 5-stage model. It includes:

- consideration of referrals for assessments from parents and schools;
- discussion of criteria used by LEAs in deciding to make a statutory assessment;
- description of stages involved in statutory assessments and SEN co-ordinator's role;

- discussion of implications of statements of SEN for SEN co-ordinator's role;
- discussion of the school's role in annual reviews of progress;
- the development of transition plans for children with SEN aged 14 to 19 years.

Chapter Six considers the use of effective strategies for involving parents in the education of their children with SEN. It includes discussion of:

- recent increases in parental rights regarding children with SEN;
- a model to guide the practice of parental involvement;
- facilitating parental involvement in assessments and reviews;
- developing a school policy for involving parents;
- competencies needed for effective parental involvement.

Chapter Seven focuses on the interpersonal skills needed by SEN co-ordinators for working with parents, outside specialists and colleagues within their school. Included are:

- listening skills such as paraphrasing and active listening;
- the counselling skills needed to use a 3-stage problem-solving model of counselling;
- assertion skills such as making requests and giving constructive feedback;
- stress management skills such as time management strategies.

Chapter Eight discusses the criteria for evaluating the effectiveness of SEN provision within the school to be used in OFSTED inspections. It focuses on:

- the questions which should be asked of the chief inspector before the inspection;
- the information on provisions for SEN which should be made available beforehand;
- the key aspects of the school's SEN provision upon which the inspection will focus;
- the criteria used by inspectors to evaluate the effectiveness of the school's SEN provision.

Chapter Nine considers some challenges for the future raised by the implemention of the Code of Practice in mainstream schools, such as:

- establishing effective school-wide identification and assessment procedures;
- establishing effective procedures for arranging provision and monitoring progress;

- developing time-efficient procedures for recording;
- developing effective consultation with parents and agencies external to the school;
- ensuring accountability of funding and resources, both human and material;
- establishing adequate pre-service and in-service training on the Code.

Finally, the *annotated bibliography* provides a list of useful resources which are relevant to the effective implementation of the Code of Practice and are considered to be particularly relevant to SEN co-ordinators in mainstream schools.

HOW TO USE THE HANDBOOK

Checklists and proformas are included throughout the handbook to help SEN co-ordinators design and implement school policy and procedures in accord with the intentions of the Code of Practice.

The handbook is presented in what the authors considered to be a logical sequence for SEN co-ordinators to work through in order to review their own school's provisions and practice with regard to SEN. However, each chapter covers a specific aspect of the Code and therefore can be read separately from the rest. This will enable SEN co-ordinators to focus on the various aspects involved in implementing the Code in any order of priority. For example, SEN co-ordinators whose priority is an OFSTED inspection may want to review Chapter Eight first. Alternatively, SEN co-ordinators who want to improve parental involvement within their schools may want to read Chapters Six and Seven first.

The major focus of the handbook is on the implementation of the Code of Practice in mainstream schools and therefore aspects most relevant to this task have been included. It was not possible to provide information about other aspects of education relevant to children with SEN such as detailed discussion of the different types of disabilities and their implications for teachers. Since this information is available elsewhere the handbook provides references to useful sources within the chapters and at the end of the book in the form of an annotated bibliography.

CHAPTER TWO

Overview of the Code of Practice

INTRODUCTION

This chapter provides an overview of the principles and requirements of the Code of Practice and the associated DfE Circular (6/94). Particular emphasis is placed on the role of the SEN co-ordinator and on the issues which need to be addressed in order to ensure an effective whole-school approach to meeting special educational needs in mainstream schools.

Principles and Practices Expounded by the Code

The Code of Practice identifies fundamental principles on which the practices and procedures for meeting special educational needs (SEN) should be based. These are that:

- the needs of all pupils with SEN of either a short-term or long-term nature must be addressed by schools;
- there is a continuum of special educational needs and a continuum of special needs provision is required in order to meet these needs (as elaborated in Chapter One);
- children with special educational needs require a broad and balanced education, including the National Curriculum;
- the needs of most pupils with SEN will be met in mainstream schools without the need for statutory assessments or statements of SEN;
- children with special educational needs, including those with statements of SEN, should, wherever possible, be educated in mainstream schools, if this

is in accord with their parents' wishes;

- pre-school children may have special educational needs which require the intervention of LEAs and health services;
- effective assessment of and provision for children with SEN depends on the development of a working partnership between parents, schools, LEAs and other agencies.

These principles are underwritten by the following set of practices and procedures:

- children with special educational needs should be identified as early as possible and an assessment of their specific needs conducted as quickly as possible;
- provision for children with special educational needs should be made in the most appropriate setting, which, in most cases, will be the child's mainstream school, without the need for statutory assessment or a statement of SEN;
- all assessment and planning for children with SEN should be conducted in partnership with their parents;
- for the minority of children with SEN who require statements of special educational needs, LEAs must complete the statementing process within the prescribed time limits; they must write clear and comprehensive statements, setting out the child's SEN and any other needs, the specific objectives to be worked towards, the SEN provision to be made and the arrangements for monitoring progress and reviewing SEN provision;
- the wishes of children with SEN, considered in the light of their ages and level of understanding, should be taken into account in determining special educational provision;
- special educational provision will be most effective where there is close co-operation between all the agencies concerned and a multi-disciplinary approach to assessment and curriculum planning.

Requirements of the Code

The Code of Practice makes it clear that there is a professional expectation that teachers and schools will be able to *provide detailed evidence* to support any discussions or action regarding children with special educational needs. This means that it is essential that schools have kept meticulously accurate records from the moment a concern was noted.

It is essential therefore that the teacher with overall responsibility for the education of children with special educational needs within a school, typically the SEN co-ordinator, must:

- be able to identify and assess those needs;
- be able to construct, monitor and evaluate learning experiences;
- be able to advise colleagues on the most appropriate teaching methods, together with the most advantageous learning environments;
- be able to implement procedures which allow for the identification, assessment and monitoring of pupils' needs and progress within the school;
- be able to respond to requests from parents and other agencies for information about children and their learning opportunities;
- be aware of all other agencies involved with children with special educational needs and understand their functions;
- establish, in co-operation with schools within the group, partnership, family or cluster (however they are described), an effective exchange of information at the time of transfer of pupils from one school to the next;
- have knowledge of the law governing special educational needs, in particular as it relates to the Children Act and the rights of parents;
- understand those sections of the Education Reform Act 1988 which relate to children with special educational needs and the National Curriculum;
- be thoroughly familiar with the Code of Practice and related documents.

It is very easy to put in writing or even embody in the law that the needs of all pupils with SEN must be addressed. *It is another matter to ensure that this is done.* Teachers currently working with pupils with SEN in mainstream schools know that it is not always possible to obtain the level of commitment from colleagues which will ensure parity of provision and equality of opportunity. It will be essential, if this Code of Practice is to be successful in improving SEN provision in mainstream schools, for attitudes, understanding and expectations of teachers to change. From our experience and observations this is easier to achieve if the teacher responsible for SEN is fully conversant with current views of what comprises effective practice, as is elaborated in the Code of Practice, and can be seen to be putting this into operation.

THE ROLE OF THE SEN CO-ORDINATOR

The Code of Practice requires that all mainstream schools have a designated SEN co-ordinator who is responsible for the day-to-day management of the school's provisions for children with SEN. This will involve: advising class and subject teachers, undertaking comprehensive assessments; providing individualised teaching programmes; arranging pupil support; overseeing and updating comprehensive records on all pupils with special educational needs in the school. The co-ordinator will also need to work closely with parents of children with SEN, as well as liaise with external agencies, which will include the educational psychology service and other support agencies, medical and social services and voluntary bodies.

The role of SEN co-ordinator is crucial in the implementation of the principles and practices of the Code of Practice. Typically, in many small primary schools the SEN co-ordinator is the head teacher or deputy, whilst in larger primary schools and secondary schools it can be a member of the senior management team or a member of staff who might be known by some other title such as 'head of special needs' or 'head of learning support'. It does appear that the role of the SEN co-ordinator as outlined in the Code is closest to the post often described as head of special needs in secondary schools. The teacher designated as SEN co-ordinator will require definite clarification of his or her role when a school is putting its arrangements in place. It is probably reasonable to assume that in most schools the person responsible for the day-to-day management of provision for children with special educational needs will be designated as SEN co-ordinator.

THE 5-STAGE MODEL FOR MEETING SEN

The Code of Practice suggests a 5-stage model for meeting special educational needs within schools, although LEAs and schools may adopt models with more or less than 5 stages. What is important is that schools should establish or adopt (usually from the LEA) a staged process which starts with the class or subject teacher and demonstrates the increasing involvement of other teachers and outside agencies until a formal assessment of a child's SEN may be made. It is clear that the expectation embodied in the Code is that the majority of children's special educational needs will be addressed by the school without the involvement of the LEA or LEA services. Where that is found to be impossible, then and only then can a school move forward to the later stages of the model. Whatever staged process is adopted by a school it must match the recommendations made within the 5-stage approach. A summary of the model which is recommended by the Code is presented in Figure 2.1. Some LEAs are advising their schools that they intend to retain the staged approach which they have already established. For example, some LEAs have 3-stage procedures, others have 4- or 6-stage procedures and still other LEAs may label the stages in different ways but the important thing is that a staged approach is used, similar to that in the Code, which is outlined below and described in more detail in Chapters Three and Four.

- *Stage 1* requires a class or subject teacher to take the initiative and register their concern in respect of a pupil's difficulties. They must then gather information from various sources and attempt to address the child's

- *Stage 1.* Class or subject teachers identify or register child's special educational needs and, consulting the school's SEN co-ordinator, take initial action.

- *Stage 2.* The school's SEN co-ordinator takes lead responsibility for managing the child's special educational provision, working with the child's teachers.

- *Stage 3.* Teachers and the SEN co-ordinator are supported by specialists from outside the school.

- *Stage 4.* The LEA consider the need for a statutory assessment and, if appropriate, make a multi-disciplinary assessment.

- *Stage 5.* The LEA consider the need for a statement of special educational needs and, if appropriate, make a statement and arrange, monitor and review provision.

Figure 2.1 The 5-stage model for meeting SEN
Source: DfE, 1994, p. 3

special educational needs by, for example, using increased differentiation of the child's work. They can consult the SEN co-ordinator for advice. At a suitable point they must review what has been achieved. This stage is crucial. Nothing should be missed or omitted. It is at this point that schools should understand that anything assessed or recorded at stage 1 may be of value to an LEA in determining whether or not to provide a statement of special educational needs, if the child progresses through the model to stage 5. Sometimes matters which at the time seem to be trivial can assume greater significance at a later date. In summary, this stage focuses on the response made by the class teacher and the class-based resources used.

- *Stage 2* is entered when it is considered that the stage 1 intervention has not had the desired effect. This is the point at which the SEN co-ordinator takes control and initiates further assessment and collects additional information. Here the co-ordinator has more information to use and more resources to draw upon. It is becoming clear that the significant difference between stages 1 and 2 is the difference between what can be done in a classroom by the class teacher with classroom resources and what can be done by the class teacher plus the co-ordinator using school-based resources and staff.

- *Stage 3* is the point at which schools consider that they need the support of outside agencies to work with them in providing advice and support which is not available within the school. Here it is envisaged that schools and agencies will work jointly together, supported by the parents, to address the child's SEN.

- *Stage 4* is the significant step of referring the pupil to the LEA for consideration of a multi-disciplinary assessment. LEAs will study any referral and determine whether or not to make such an assessment.
- *Stage 5* comes into effect once a multi-disciplinary assessment has been made. It is at this point where it is decided whether or not a statement should be written.

It is important that schools make effective provision for the management of stages 1–3 which includes rigorous and effective record keeping in order to provide the evidence which may be required by the LEA. Schools must have an understanding of what will happen in stages 4 and 5 although the management of them will be outside their control.

ISSUES TO BE ADDRESSED

Although all the stages will be dealt with at length in later chapters it may be useful at this point to highlight some of the questions which will need to be addressed at each of the school-based stages. These are the kinds of questions which Inspectors may ask either on a routine visit or an official inspection.

Stage 1
Questions to be answered include:

1 How is the registration of concern about a pupil made and to whom? In some schools it will be the head teacher, in others the SEN co-ordinator, in others a head of year.
2 What procedure has the school established if the concern is registered by a parent or other professional?
3 What happens when the concern has been registered? Is it recorded? If so how? What is done with the information?
4 Who collects and collates the information which the Code recommends is collected at this stage?
5 Who will meet with the parents to discuss concerns? Head teacher? Class teacher? SEN co-ordinator?
6 What is recorded at the meeting and how?
7 To whom is the information given?
8 Where is it stored?
9 How is the information to be used so that suitable arrangements can be

made to address the pupil's needs.

10 Once appropriate action has been determined how will the class teacher carry it out?

11 From where is the time found to put these procedures into practice? (See Chapter Seven.)

Stage 2

Questions to be answered include:

1 Does the SEN co-ordinator have the time and opportunity to assume this lead role?

2 Does the school have the resources to undertake a comprehensive range of assessments?

3 How will this lead role dovetail with other management systems in the school? For example, the pastoral network.

4 Where are the records kept?

5 How is the Individual Education Plan (IEP) going to be written?

6 How will the IEP be monitored?

7 Who manages the support systems within the school?

8 Is the withdrawal of pupils for individual or small group tuition an option in the school?

Stage 3

Questions to be answered include:

1 Does the SEN co-ordinator know where specialist services are based, how to contact them and by what means? For example, is a form to be completed? Is a phone call sufficient?

2 Is the documentation from stages 1 and 2 readily available for the specialist agency?

3 Are roles and responsibilities clearly understood by all concerned?

4 Has a timescale for action been drawn up and agreement reached as to 'who does what'?

5 Is regular monitoring by the specialist services part of the agreement?

6 Has a review date been agreed and a list of people to attend the meeting been drawn up?

The consideration of such questions underscores the necessity for having a policy and procedures for SEN which are agreed across the whole school.

DEVELOPING A WHOLE-SCHOOL POLICY FOR SEN

The Education Act 1993 determined that all schools must formulate and publish an SEN policy which should be available to parents. Guidelines regarding what should be included in this policy are provided by the Code of Practice (p. 8) and DfE Circular 6/94 (pp. 10–20). These guidelines are summarised and discussed briefly below.

Aims and objectives.   The guiding principles which determine the provisions which schools will make for children with SEN must be included in their SEN policy, together with the objectives through which they will develop those provisions.

Designated teacher.   The name of the teacher who is the designated SEN co-ordinator (possibly together with his/her qualifications and experience) should be included. This must be the person who is responsible for the operation of SEN provision within the school on a day-to-day basis.

Co-ordination arrangements.   The policy must specify which member(s) of staff are responsible for putting the school's SEN policy into operation. This will involve liaising with other teachers, parents and outside specialists, keeping adequate records including an SEN register and overall co-ordination of the school's SEN provision. Typically, the SEN co-ordinator will have this responsibility but in some schools, particularly larger second-ary schools, the responsibilities may be shared. For example, one school actually splits the co-ordination of stages 1 and 2 and stages 3, 4 and 5 between two members of staff. The named co-ordinator covers stages 1 and 2 and the deputy head covers 3, 4 and 5. The whole process is managed by a team of three who meet on a regular basis, namely the head, the deputy and the SEN co-ordinator.

Admission arrangements.   The policy should state whether any priority is given to the admission of pupils with SEN who do not have statements. For example, does the school have a reputation for specialising in pupils with specific learning difficulties, or does access to its various facilities make it particularly suitable for children with physical disabilities?

SEN specialisms.   The policy must describe any special facilities which the school has or indeed any special expertise which it can offer. For example, if the school has a special unit for children with sensory difficulties, the operation of this unit should be described and staff qualifications and experience noted. Alternatively, if the school has built up experience of catering for children with moderate learning difficulties in mainstream classes the arrangement made for this should be briefly described.

Accessibility. It is clearly desirable that as many pupils as possible can attend their local school. The SEN policy must therefore describe such things as access to the school and the curriculum for children with disabilities, including wheelchair access, soundproofing of rooms and special lighting provided.

Resource allocation. The policy must explain the principles by which resources are allocated to pupils with special needs. Many maintained schools have funding that reflects the incidence of pupils with SEN, which is allocated through LMS devolvement. This needs to be made clear in the policy, as does the formula by which such a figure has been arrived at. Schools who have pupils with statements of SEN may receive funding which is associated with the provision highlighted on the statement. The policy should explain the process by which such funding is allocated and monitored.

Organisation of SEN provision. A substantial section of the school's SEN policy must describe how the school manages the staged procedures discussed within the Code of Practice. It should describe the systems for identifying, assessing, monitoring and reviewing pupils with special educational needs within the school. This section will provide detailed information about what happens at each stage, including how a concern is registered, what happens then and what records are kept (see Chapters Three, Four and Five).

Curriculum access. How the school will provide pupils with SEN with a broad, balanced and relevant curriculum, including the National Curriculum, should be stated in the policy. This section should take into account how the school's curriculum development meets the needs of pupils with SEN, together with details of the range of teaching strategies, differentiation and special arrangements such as in-class support and withdrawal for individual or small group tuition.

Integration. It is expected that pupils with SEN will participate in school activities with pupils who do not have special educational needs. The policy should describe all situations in which this occurs such as school assemblies, playtimes and meal times. Schools may find that far from describing 'integration' situations, it may be easier to describe those special occasions when some pupils are withdrawn for additional work, either individually or in a small group. Many schools want their pupils with special needs to be part of a normal class situation and 'integration' is not an issue for them to address, rather the reverse.

Evaluation. Arrangements for the evaluation of the school's procedures and practices with regard to SEN provision should be included in the policy. Here schools may wish to highlight certain criteria or targets against which the success of their work can be measured. Some LEAs refer to these as 'performance indicators'.

Handling complaints. Arrangements for making and dealing with complaints should be described. This section should include the details of how the school will investigate and handle such a complaint. Those details should include a timescale for action so that a parent can understand what should be happening and when.

Staff training. The school's plans for the in-service training and professional development of its staff should be described in the policy. This section can include information as to how the school will take advantage of any LEA training programmes which will be of use to its SEN co-ordinator, other teachers and non-teaching staff as well as any collaborative arrangements for training with other schools.

Outside support. Arrangements for gaining the assistance of outside agencies and support services should be noted. In fact, it would be helpful to include the names and contact arrangements for all support services available through the LEA as well as the social service department, health authority and other agencies which are frequently consulted.

Partnership with parents. The policy should contain a clear description of the school's arrangements for developing a close working relationship with the parents of pupils in the school (see Chapter Six).

Links with other schools. The SEN policy should outline any arrangements whereby the school draws upon expertise from special schools, units or other special provision. Details of those arrangements, which might include part-time attendance for pupils, need to be explained. Also included needs to be the links with feeder schools and arrangements for when pupils change schools.

Links with outside agencies. This section of the policy should outline the arrangements schools have made for liaison with outside agencies such as social services, the health authority, the education welfare service and any voluntary organisations either locally or nationally.

Developing the Policy

The SEN policy should be determined by the governing body of the school in consultation with the head teacher. In some schools this responsibility is delegated to the SEN co-ordinator. In others the governing body will appoint a sub-committee to work with the head teacher and SEN co-ordinator. Whatever the arrangements, time should be found for consultation with all staff, parents and other agencies. This could be managed by the SEN co-ordinator by arranging consultative documents to aid staff meetings and departmental discussions. Any policy which has been subjected to substantial discussion, regular review and modification, though time consuming in its formulation, is likely to have the support and commitment of staff who have to work within its confines.

Focusing on the management of change within schools, Gross (1993) presents a 4-step model for the development of a whole-school policy for SEN.

- *Step 1: Reviewing current practice* involves obtaining the views of teachers, governors, parents, pupils and specialists who come into the school regarding the school's strengths and weaknesses in its provision for SEN.
- *Step 2: Developing a vision* involves elaborating the values, principles and practices which the school would want to adhere to. This is where the guidance provided by the Code of Practice, which was discussed above, is useful.
- *Step 3: Comparing vision and practice* involves considering the vision in terms of the school's current practice of provision for SEN. Gross suggests that the school staff, either individually or in groups, are asked to list areas of the school's current practice regarding SEN which are in accord with this vision and to identify gaps in their provision which need to be prioritised for development.
- *Step 4: Drafting the policy* involves producing a draft of the whole school policy for SEN which has been informed by the work done in the preceding three steps.

Fully involving staff in this 4-step process not only facilitates their commitment to the final form of the policy but also increases their awareness of its contents and aspects of the school's provision for SEN which need attention.

Governors

Governors have a responsibility to produce an annual report which will state the number of pupils with special educational needs in the school and comment on the school's effectiveness in the following areas:

1   identification of needs;
2   assessment of needs;
3   provision for meeting special educational needs;
4   methods for monitoring and record keeping;
5   the use made by the school of outside agencies and support services.

It is essential for a governing body to appoint a named governor, or a sub-committee of governors, to take responsibility for SEN. They must oversee the school's arrangements, and report back to the governing body. Clearly, it is important for the SEN co-ordinator to liaise as closely as possible with the governor responsible for SEN. In some schools this liaison would be through the head teacher, in others it would be direct (Scott, 1993).

SUMMARY AND CONCLUSIONS

This chapter has provided an overview of the principles and practices espoused by the Code of Practice and focused on some of the expectations embodied within the first 3 stages of the 5-stage model. Schools should ensure that there is a clearly understood policy and procedures for the implementation of the model and that this is strictly followed for any child with special educational needs. Record keeping, and the production of evidence to support any decisions or action are crucial and every effort should be made to see that these are regularly and meticulously completed. Most schools will need to undertake a review of the roles and responsibilities of staff and provide the opportunities for the requirements of the staged model to be efficiently undertaken. Chapter Three will provide more detailed guidance together with examples from schools.

CHAPTER THREE

Using the School's Resources to Meet SEN at Stages 1 and 2

PROVISIONS FOR SEN AT STAGE 1

Stage 1 of the Code of Practice is concerned with identifying and registering a child's special educational needs and taking action to meet those needs within the normal classroom situation. The trigger for this stage is an 'expression of concern that a child is showing signs of having special educational needs' (DfE, 1994, p. 23). This can be made by the parents, a teacher or another professional such as a health or social services worker. Evidence has to be produced to substantiate the expression of concern. As far as the school is concerned this should be provided by a range of indicators including such things as a basic concepts checklist (often used in primary and infant schools), National Curriculum attainments and standardised test and screening procedures for aspects of learning such as reading, spelling, mathematical skills and cognitive ability. (A list of major publishers who produce a wide range of testing materials can be found on page 150). It has to be recognised that each school will have its own favoured methods of identifying children who potentially have special needs and that there is no need to radically alter current practices if they are appropriate and reliable.

The expression of concern at this stage would normally be made to the child's class teacher in the primary phase or to the form tutor or the year tutor in the secondary phase. Once made the expression of concern must be acted upon. A form that could be used within a school to register an expression of concern is presented in the Appendices as A1. The person who is expressing the concern completes the form identifying the child and giving the reason for that concern. In a primary school this concern could be that a child has poor physical co-ordination and is unable to perform accurately the sorts of simple tasks that are age appropriate for that child. National Curriculum Key Stage assessment results could also be the trigger of an expression of concern.

At stage 1 there are four main aspects of SEN provision which need to be considered. These are:

- the roles and responsibilities of the staff involved with the child;
- the information that is required;
- the assessment of and provision for the child's needs; and
- reviews of progress.

These aspects are discussed in detail below.

Roles and Responsibilities

At this stage the class teacher, the form tutor or the teacher with responsibility for the year, as appropriate, takes overall responsibility for the child's educational programme and has to inform the head teacher, the SEN co-ordinator and the parents that the child is being considered under stage 1 of the Code of Practice. Although the needs of the majority of children will be met at stages 1, 2 and 3, it is important that parents should understand the implications that could arise from following the procedures through to a possible conclusion at stage 5. It is, therefore, advisable to meet with parents at this stage allowing sufficient time for a full discussion of both the implications and the parents' concerns and ideas.

The SEN co-ordinator is expected to offer advice and support as necessary to both the teachers and parents concerned. This could include helping to gather the necessary information required, helping to assess the child's needs and advising and supporting the child's teachers on such matters as teaching methods and materials or suggestions of how work might best be differentiated. At this stage the provision will make use of the materials and resources that are available for use within the child's classroom as part of normal teaching arrangements.

However, the overall responsibility for collecting all the necessary information and making the initial assessment of the child's special educational needs lies with the child's teacher or tutor (see the following section for details).

Having collected all the relevant information the teacher or tutor will need to hold an initial meeting to consider what action it would be appropriate to take. The SEN co-ordinator and the parents of the child should be involved in the discussions. If it is agreed at this meeting that the child is experiencing difficulties the teacher or tutor is required to provide additional help within the child's normal teaching framework, using teaching strategies, resources and differentiation of work in order to meet the child's needs more effectively.

It is also important to set out who will be responsible for monitoring the additional help given, how it will be monitored and how frequently. In the example of the child with poor physical co-ordination given previously the monitoring could be carried out by the class teacher by observing the child completing tasks set by the teacher in order to improve the child's co-ordination, on a weekly basis. The date for a meeting of the teacher, the SEN co-ordinator and parents (if appropriate), to review this extra help, should also be agreed. A sample proforma for recording this meeting and the outcome is presented in the Appendices as A2.

The SEN co-ordinator also has to ensure that a record of action is started in respect of the child and to include the child on the school's SEN register. There are obvious implications for record keeping including the need to avoid unnecessary duplication or bureaucracy. It may be advisable for the SEN co-ordinator to keep separate individual files for pupils identified with SEN in addition to normal school records. A sample log sheet, which could be used to record the actions taken concerning an individual child, is presented in the Appendices as A3.

Information Required

The information that the child's teacher should collect and record at stage 1 includes information from the school, the parents, the child and, possibly, other sources.

Information required from the school
All records that are held by the school should be used to inform the process. These will include the following:

1   All current and past class records. Records from any other school(s) the child has attended in the previous year should also be available. These records will include the statutory annual report to parents as well as any informal contacts that have been made. It is essential that all contacts with parents during a child's school career should be recorded as they might become important evidence if the child progresses further through the 5-stage procedure.
2   Any data available concerning National Curriculum attainments, both teacher assessments and statutory assessments.
3   Any standardised test results, profiles of attainment or screening test assessments.
4   Any school Records of Achievement data.
5   Any reports on the pupil in school settings, which could come from a

variety of sources, including teachers, dinner supervisors, or the school first-aider.

6 Any observations about the child's behaviour which could again come from a wide variety of sources and apply to a wide variety of school activities.

7 Any known health or social problems which have been identified by the parents and about which the school has been informed.

Information required from the parents

The information obtained from parents, or those with parental responsibility, will include the following:

1 Additional information and views on the child's health and general development which could be relevant to the child's progress, including medical conditions, medication taken and, perhaps, even pre-natal conditions.

2 Parents' perceptions of how their child is performing and behaving while at school and the progress being made.

3 Parents' perceptions of their child's progress and behaviour in the home situation.

4 Any additional factors which parents believe may be contributing to the difficulties being experienced.

5 Parents' opinions about the sorts of actions that the school could be taking and provision that would be necessary.

Information required from the child

Obtaining information from the child will need to be handled sensitively and will probably best be done in conjunction with the parents. It is possible that there will be circumstances in which it may not be possible to obtain information from the child. These circumstances are most likely to apply to the very young and those with poor communication skills or levels of comprehension. The information which should be sought from the child includes:

1 The child's personal perception of any difficulties that he or she is experiencing.

2 How the child would like these difficulties to be addressed.

Information from other sources

Information which could be obtained from other sources will include that which is already available to the school from sources such as health services, the education welfare service and social services. It is important that records are kept of the information-collecting process, including what information is being requested with dates. A sample proforma for this purpose is presented in the Appendices as A4.

Assessment of and Provision for the Child's Needs

The information that has been gathered at this stage is designed to focus on:

1   the different perceptions that are held by those people who are directly concerned with the child;
2   the immediate educational concerns of those people;
3   the learning difficulties of the child as seen in a wider context.

Once all the relevant information has been gathered together the teacher or tutor, in consultation with the SEN co-ordinator, then has to decide on the course of action to be followed. There are three alternatives:

1   to continue with the existing arrangements for the child with no special help being required;
2   to seek additional advice and/or support;
3   to give additional help to the child through appropriate differentiation of the curriculum, co-operative learning arrangements where the teacher carefully selects the group in which the child will work, small group teaching or the provision of materials to help understanding. Such arrangements have to be monitored and reviewed on a regular basis, evaluating the progress made.

Continuing existing arrangements

It may be that, as a result of the procedures that have been followed so far, the problem has been resolved and no further action is necessary. Any such conclusion should be recorded and form part of the school's records that are kept on the child and on the SEN procedures. The child's parents and the SEN co-ordinator must be informed of the decision to continue with existing arrangements. The co-ordinator is required to retain the child's name on the SEN register and to consult with the teacher or tutor on a regular basis (typically termly or 6-monthly) until it is clear that the child's progress is not likely to give cause for concern.

Seeking additional advice and/or support

It may be obvious from the beginning of the process that additional information is required for a decision to be made. This information may have to come from one or more of the support services or specialist agencies (see Chapter Four for details). Equally, it may be obvious that action at stage 1 would be inadequate and not resolve the problem. Under these circumstances the child should be moved to the appropriate stage.

Giving special help at stage 1

Having consulted with the SEN co-ordinator, the teacher or tutor may decide that it would be beneficial for the child to have special attention for a period of time. Typically this would take the form of appropriately differentiating the teaching and/or set work for the child within the classroom setting. The nature and aims of such special attention should be recorded, including the nature of the concern expressed, the action that is to be taken, the targets to be achieved, the arrangements for monitoring the process and a review date. In addition, parents should be encouraged to help their child at home and advice given to them by the teacher as to what form of help would be most beneficial and effective. An example of a proforma which might be used for this purpose is presented in the Appendices as A5.

When initially completing the proforma, the class teacher, form or year tutor, in consultation with the SEN co-ordinator, fills in the details in section 1, section 2 and section 3. Section 1 identifies the child concerned, the dates of the plan and its review, the circulation to others who are involved in the teaching of the child within the school and those people who will be involved in the review meeting. Section 2 outlines the reasons for concern about the child's learning. Detailed evidence which supports this concern will be held elsewhere in the record-keeping system and it will only be necessary to refer to this evidence in this section. Section 3 outlines the special provision that will be made, the targets that are to be achieved and the arrangements for monitoring the provision and progress.

The date when the proforma should be returned by teaching staff to the class teacher, form or year teacher should also be completed. This will be shortly before the review date so that information can be collated to inform that review.

When this has been completed, a copy of the proforma is given to all those people identified on the circulation list in section 1. Members of staff who teach the child concerned will need to take appropriate action to implement the provision in their lessons. In a primary school this will probably concern only a small number of staff, whereas in a secondary school considerably more teachers will be involved.

Section 4 is completed by those staff who teach the child shortly before the

Wonder Road _____ SCHOOL
ADDITIONAL HELP AT STAGE 1

SECTION 1
NAME: James Truggles FORM: 3C DATE OF BIRTH: 15/10/85
DATE OF PLAN: 1/10/94 REVIEW DATE: 1/12/94
CIRCULATION: PARENTS, HEAD, SEN CO-ORDINATOR, OTHERS ___
PEOPLE TO BE INVOLVED IN THE REVIEW: PARENTS, SEN CO-ORDINATOR,
OTHERS ___

SECTION 2
REASONS FOR IDENTIFICATION: James' spelling is not developing at
the expected rate. At KS2 he achieved Level 2
and a recent teacher assessment puts him at the
same level. His results on the Spar Spelling test
was 82. James has particular difficulties with magic e
words and simple digraphs

SECTION 3
ACTION TO BE TAKEN: To concentrate on particular aspects of
spelling beginning with the magic e rule by (1) concentrating
on exercises using magic e (2) small group work on magic e (3) using
follow-up exercises for parents to give at home (4) monitoring all
spelling in written work.
TARGETS: To obtain two consecutive test results on the magic
e rule with no mistakes.

MONITORING ARRANGEMENTS: _____
    (1) to check all spellings in written work

    (2) to administer tests on a weekly basis from
        22/10/94

SECTION 4
REVIEW (including progress made with evidence where appropriate): _____
    James has responded well to the programme of work
    He achieved the target set after 3 tests (attached). He has
    also demonstrated the correct use of the magic e rule
    in his general writing.

RECOMMENDATIONS FOR FUTURE ACTION: _____
(1) to continue with a similar programme to deal with gh and ght
digraphs (2) to continue to monitor the spelling of magic e
words.

SIGNED: _____ (class teacher) DATE: 27/11/94

PLEASE COMPLETE THE REVIEW SECTION ABOVE WHEN APPROPRIATE AND RETURN
THIS FORM TO ___ A Parson ___ BY 28/11/94

Figure 3.1 Completed proforma for giving help at stage 1

review date. They should outline the progress or otherwise that the child has made in the area of concern within the review period in their lessons. This represents a comment on the effectiveness of the provision. In addition, staff should make recommendations for any future action that they consider to be necessary to address the child's difficulties.

Having gathered the information provided by teaching staff, the class teacher, form or year tutor, with the SEN co-ordinator, can assess the progress made and complete the summary of progress section on the review proforma, prior to the review meeting. This will be a much simpler process in a primary school compared to a secondary school because of the numbers of staff involved. An example of a completed proforma for giving help at stage 1 is presented at Figure 3.1.

Review of Progress

Reviews should focus on the effectiveness of the special help that has been given and the progress that has been made by the child. It should also consider what future course of action should be followed. Teachers may take advantage of the school's normal consultation arrangements, such as parents' evenings, to enable parents to contribute to reviews of progress at stage 1. An example of a completed proforma which might be used for the review at stage 1 is presented at Figure 3.2 and a blank version is shown in the Appendices as A6.

The outcome of the review may be:

1 *The child no longer needs special help.* This will apply if the child's progress remains satisfactory for at least two review periods. The child's name should still be retained on the SEN register and reviewed until it is clear that progress is unlikely to be a cause for future concern.
2 *The child continues at stage 1.* This will apply if the child's progress has been at least satisfactory in terms of meeting the targets that were set. New targets should now be set which should be achieved by the next review. If the progress made remains satisfactory for two review periods it may be decided to gradually increase the time span between the reviews.
3 *The child moves to stage 2.* This will apply when the child has failed to make satisfactory progress after up to two review periods of receiving special help from his or her teacher.

It would be helpful to have some criteria for defining what constitutes unsatisfactory progress. This might involve consideration of progress made in relation to the pupil's age, the progress made by peers, the speed at which

Wonder Road SCHOOL
REVIEW OF HELP GIVEN AT STAGE 1
REVIEW NO. _____

NAME: _James Truggles_ FORM: _8C_ DATE OF BIRTH: _15/10/85_
DATE OF REVIEW: _1/12/94_
PRESENT: _Mr & Mrs L. Truggles, James Truggles Mrs Hawkes (SENCO), A Dean_

1. SUMMARY OF PROGRESS MADE: _James successfully completed the programme & appears to have mastered the rule concerned with magic e. His general writing has very few magic e mistakes_

2. VIEWS OF PARENT: _Very pleased with James' achievements. They have noticed an improvement with his spelling._

3. VIEWS OF CHILD: _James is pleased with his improvement in spelling. Enjoyed getting 10/10 for his tests._

4. EFFECTIVENESS OF PLAN: _The plan was felt to be an effective way of dealing with the problem. Parents were willing to continue to give help._

5. UPDATED/ADDITIONAL INFORMATION: _None_

6. FUTURE ACTION: (please tick as appropriate)
(a) No further action
(b) Continue at stage 1 ✓ _– Deal with digraphs gh, ght._
(c) Move to stage 2

RECOMMENDATIONS FOR IEP AT STAGE 2: (if appropriate) _____
_N/A_

SIGNED: _L. Truggles_ _____ (parent)
James Truggles _____ (child if appropriate)
_____ (class/year teacher)

Figure 3.2 Completed proforma for use at a review at stage 1

progress is made or the progress made in relation to the additional help given. For example, a child who is following a structured reading scheme to develop reading skills might be considered to be making unsatisfactory progress if the gap between his or her chronological age and reading age increases or, the speed at which a child is able to progress through a project designed for a whole class is significantly slower than his or her peers even though the work has been appropriately differentiated for that child.

An example of a completed proforma for the review of help given at stage 1 is presented at Figure 3.2. Only the section concerned with the details of the child concerned, the date of the review meeting and the school's summary of the progress made can be completed beforehand. All the other sections will be completed at the meeting. If it is decided that further action is necessary, either at stage 1 or stage 2, then sections of the appropriate proforma for that stage can be completed (see A5, A7 and A8 in the Appendices), thus saving time and simplifying the procedures.

If parents are unable to attend the review meeting they must be informed of the outcome of the review. If it is decided to move the child on to stage 2 of the procedures then it is important to talk with them in person.

PROVISIONS FOR SEN AT STAGE 2

The main change that occurs at stage 2 is that the SEN co-ordinator takes overall responsibility for the assessment of the child's learning difficulties and then planning, monitoring and reviewing the special educational provision that is made, working in conjunction with the child's teacher(s). As part of this process it is necessary to prepare an Individual Education Plan (IEP) (see Butt and Scott, 1994, for a useful discussion of IEP rationale).

The trigger for moving a child to stage 2 is either:

- the decision that resulted from the review at stage 1; or
- the SEN co-ordinator considers that early intervention is appropriate as a result of the information obtained and the discussions held at the time of the initial expression of concern.

The information-gathering process is much the same as at stage 1. The need for effective systems of assessment, recording and monitoring becomes increasingly important, both in terms of using information from stage 1 and the efficient use of time. If effective recording and monitoring systems are developed, each stage should be efficiently informed by the stage before and a comprehensive range of documentation built up if a child progresses through stages 1 to 3 to a formal assessment at stage 4.

The SEN co-ordinator must review all the information already gathered at stage 1. Information should always be sought from other professionals or agencies involved with the child at this stage. Sources could include:

1   The school doctor or the child's GP, for relevant medical advice, providing that permission has first been obtained from the parents.
2   Social services or the education welfare service. This information could be on:
    (a) any arrangements which are part of an education supervision order;
    (b) any involvement that the social services may have with the child or the family;
    (c) any concerns that there may be about the child's welfare;
    (d) whether the child is on any local authority 'at risk' or child protection register;
    (e) if the local authority has any responsibilities for the child under the Children Act.

The SEN co-ordinator is also entitled to seek additional information from any other agencies which might be closely involved with the child. Such agencies can include any organisation which is outside the normal school provision or which is voluntary in nature with which the child is involved, such as those agencies that provide leisure activities or act as support groups for parents who have children with particular disabilities.

All this has been summarised in an 'information checklist'. A suggested format for this is given in the Appendices as A4 and could be kept as part of the recording process for individual children (see section on stage 1).

Having gathered all the relevant information together the SEN co-ordinator has to decide whether to seek further advice and/or whether to draw up an Individual Education Plan.

Seeking Further Advice

The SEN co-ordinator should seek further advice if the information that has been obtained indicates that a more detailed investigation of any area of the child's performance or development is warranted. In such circumstances the co-ordinator must record:

- what further advice is being requested;
- what arrangements will be made for the child whilst that information is being obtained;
- the review arrangements once the information has been received.

The Individual Education Plan (IEP)

The course of action that is to be followed with the child must be set out in an Individual Education Plan that is drawn up by the SEN co-ordinator in consultation with the child's class teacher or form/year tutor and any relevant curriculum specialists. It is recommended that the child's parents are also involved in this process. The information contained in this plan will be made available to everyone involved in the education of that child.

As far as is possible the plan should build on the curriculum that the child is already following, along with his or her peers. It is important that the plan should be implemented as much as possible within the classroom and make use of the programmes, activities, resources and assessment techniques that are available to the child's teacher(s). It is therefore essential that the co-ordinator ensures that there is a close liaison between all teachers who have contact with the child.

The Code of Practice (page 28) identifies seven areas that must be addressed in the IEP. These are:

1   *The nature of the learning difficulties identified.* This could range from a general difficulty that will affect learning across the whole curriculum to a specific problem that may be resolved relatively quickly.

2   *The action that is going to be taken.* This comprises the special educational provision that the school will make on behalf of the child. It should identify:

   (a) *the staff who will be involved*, and the amount and frequency of any additional support that will be provided. For example, in a secondary school, a member of the school's learning support or SEN staff might be involved with in-class support work with the child in all English lessons; in a primary school the child might be withdrawn from the class for 15 minutes at the start of each day for the SEN co-ordinator to work on a reading recovery programme;

   (b) *details of the specific programmes*, including the activities, materials and equipment, that will be utilised. In the primary example given above the programme could involve reading recovery techniques using an identified reading scheme such as Fuzzbuzz, Wellington Square or Duncan Dragon, and the associated workbooks. Alternatively, a spelling programme could involve the use of a particular computer program to assist the learning process: or a pencil grip might be needed to help a pupil with fine motor control for writing and drawing.

3   *Any help that the parents will give the child at home.* This could range from monitoring or helping with an aspect of the work. For example, spelling using a scheme provided by the school or regular paired reading,

or following a particular physical activity to help with a programme designed to improve co-ordination.

4   *The targets that are to be achieved in a given timespan.* These targets will be used at the time of the review to assess the amount of progress made. It is essential that such targets should be realistically achievable both in the time allotted and in relation to the child's ability.

5   *Any additional pastoral care arrangements or medical requirements.* For example, arrangements to enable a child to overcome a personal hygiene problem by having a shower at the start of the school day with shampoo, soap and deodorant provided, or by making laundry and ironing facilities available. Specific arrangements may have to be made for the diabetic child who has to administer injections during the school day so that this can be done in private. (NB. All schools should have a policy on the safe keeping and administration of all forms of medication.)

6   *The monitoring and assessment arrangements that will be used.* The frequency of monitoring is important as well as how that monitoring will be carried out. Monitoring may need to be on a daily or even lesson-to-lesson basis when a child's behaviour is the cause for concern. The way the behaviour is monitored may be through teacher observation and recording on an appropriate form which identifies those aspects of the child's behaviour which is being monitored. Alternatively, spelling can be monitored on a weekly basis whereas reading skills will probably require a longer timespan before significant progress can be detected. In certain cases the assessment arrangements may have to be different from the rest of the class. This would be necessary, for example, where reading skills are too low to enable the child to read a test paper, or spelling or handwriting difficulties make alternative forms of recording necessary.

7   *The arrangements and date for the review of the plan.* This should aim to include everyone who will be involved in the review meeting. The review date may be within a term or be 6 months or 1 year. This will be dependent upon the type of programme that is being implemented. A spelling or reading programme will need to run for at least a term before progress could reasonably be identified. Alternatively, a behaviour programme may require a review to be held within half a term because of the short-term goals which need to be incorporated into the programme.

Examples of proformas which could be used for this purpose are presented in the Appendices as A7, for a primary school, and A8, for a secondary school.

However, it is recognised that schools will probably wish to design their own IEP format to suit their own particular situations and needs. The proformas presented here are merely examples which could easily be adapted. Indeed, some LEAs may develop their own proformas to be used in all their schools in order to standardise procedures and information systems.

THE IEP PROFORMA

The only difference between the proforma presented for a primary school and that presented for a secondary school is in the circulation list of the plan. In a secondary school each member of staff who has a teaching responsibility for the child will have to be identified and provided with a copy. The completion of the proformas and the procedures for dealing with the administration involved is the same in both cases.

Figure 3.3 gives an example of a completed IEP proforma that might be used by a primary school with a child who is experiencing difficulty with spelling. Figure 3.4 gives an example of a completed proforma for a similar problem in a secondary school.

Sections 1, 2 and 4 are completed by the SEN co-ordinator, who will also fill in the details concerning the return of the form by the class or subject teachers, before the plan is circulated to those people identified in section 1. This could probably be done at the review meeting (of the help given at stage 1) when the decision of the review is to move to stage 2.

Sections 1 and 2 are the same format as the proforma for giving help at stage 1. Section 4 deals with the learning objectives, the criteria for success, the teaching arrangements, the additional resources and the monitoring arrangements in more detail. In the primary school example, the role of the SEN co-ordinator, in the testing procedure as well as delivery of individual teaching through withdrawal arrangements on a regular basis, is identified. The specialist resources that will be available, for both the withdrawal work and classroom use, are also identified. Parental roles in the delivery of the programme should be included where appropriate.

On receipt of the plan, the class teacher or subject teacher should complete section 5. This is the staff action plan and is the record of how the individual teacher will incorporate the programme outlined in his or her normal teaching arrangements for the child concerned. It may not be appropriate that all parts of section 5 are completed but it needs to demonstrate how the child's problem will be addressed by the individual teacher. Hence in the secondary example given, the teacher concerned is going to listen to James read using the class text on a regular basis, to highlight the technical terms that are important to the understanding of the subject to develop the correct spelling and to generally monitor all written work for spelling accuracy. A check will also be made to ensure that James wears his glasses in lessons.

Towards the end of the review period the class or subject teacher will complete section 3. This is a review of the effectiveness of the programme and

_____Wonder Road_____ SCHOOL

INDIVIDUAL EDUCATION PLAN
STAGE 2

SECTION 1

NAME: James Thuggles FORM: 8L DATE OF BIRTH: 15 / 10 /85

DATE OF PLAN: 5 /11 /95 REVIEW DATE: 5/5/96

CIRCULATION*: PARENTS, HEAD, CLASS TEACHER, OTHERS
_____

PEOPLE TO BE INVOLVED IN THE REVIEW: PARENTS, SEN CO-ORDINATOR,
OTHERS _____

SECTION 2

REASONS FOR IDENTIFICATION: Spelling - James has not made satisfactory progress over the last two review periods at stage 1. He did not achieve the targets set. Teacher assessment of NC spelling places James at level 2. There is little evidence that he is transferring the learning to other written work.

SECTION 3

REVIEW (including progress made with evidence where appropriate): James has made steady progress. He has not always shown great enthusiasm for his spelling work, but his written work has fewer mistakes than before. He is beginning to think about his mistakes and correct them. Average test mark now 6/10 compared to 5/10 previously.

RECOMMENDATIONS FOR FUTURE ACTION: James needs to continue with a similar programme, concentrating on digraphs to develop basic spelling competences

SIGNED: _____ (class teacher) DATE: 27/4/96

PLEASE COMPLETE THE REVIEW SECTION ABOVE WHEN APPROPRIATE AND
RETURN THIS FORM TO Mrs J. White (SENCO) BY 1 /5/96

Figure 3.3 Completed proforma for an IEP at stage 2 in a primary school

Figure 3.3 continued

SECTION 4

1. CURRICULAR NEEDS

(a) Priorities: *Spelling*

(b) Learning objectives: *(1) to master spelling of simple digraphs (2) to transfer skills to other writing*

(c) Criteria for success: *(1) all correct spellings on successive texts (2) improvement of spelling in written work*

(d) Monitoring and review arrangements: *(1) testing to be carried out by SENCO (2) Monitoring by class teachers of spelling in all written work*

2. TEACHING ARRANGEMENTS

(a) Strategies and techniques: *(1) Withdrawal work with SENCO for 15 mins /day (2) Specific spelling work in class (3) Parents to reinforce spelling at home*

(b) Equipment and materials: *(1) Use of SLAB Computer Programme, Use of Dorean Scheme (2) Blackwells Spelling*

3. NON-CURRICULAR NEEDS

(a) Pastoral care arrangements: *N/A*

(b) Medical requirements: *N/A*

SECTION 5

STAFF ACTION PLAN*

(a)

(b) *to concentrate on those digraphs in the class Spelling Scheme*

(c) *(1) to test regularly (2) to discuss spelling in his work*

(d) *(2) to check all written work for spelling mistakes.*

(a) *(2) regular use of spelling activities (3) provide work for parents.*

(b) ✓

(a)

(b)

Notes

NB. Section 4 is to be completed by the SEN co-ordinator before this plan is circulated.

*Staff identified in section 1 who have a teaching role with the pupil should complete section 5 on receipt of this plan.

_____ BELVIEW _____ SCHOOL

INDIVIDUAL EDUCATION PLAN

STAGE 2

SECTION 1

NAME: *JAMES TRUGGLES* FORM: *7 MD* DATE OF BIRTH: *15 / 10 / 85*

DATE OF PLAN: *10/10/97* REVIEW DATE: *1 / 5 / 98*

CIRCULATION*: PARENTS, HEAD, CLASS TEACHER, OTHERS

AN, DN, PT, MK, EM, LM, GL, LA, WA, WE, CO, RU,

PEOPLE TO BE INVOLVED IN THE REVIEW: PARENTS, SEN CO-ORDINATOR,

OTHERS *TJ (Head of Year)*

SECTION 2

REASONS FOR IDENTIFICATION: *James was identified as having a difficulty with spelling on transfer and was at Stage 2 in his primary school. Screening assessments indicate a spelling score of 82 (Vernon) and a literacy score of 84 (Spooner). Tested reading age is 9 yrs 6 mths (Neale) – 2½ years below his chronological age. He is showing signs of having difficulty with school texts.*

SECTION 3

REVIEW (including progress made with evidence where appropriate): *James' reading has improved – especially in his recognition and accurate reading of the technical words connected with this subject. The standard of his work has improved since the text has been differentiated for him. Spelling of technical terms is usually accurate. Spelling errors still abound in his work. He probably works too quickly.*

RECOMMENDATIONS FOR FUTURE ACTION: _____

Continue with a similar programme. Encourage him to slow down and give more thought to spelling and presentation.

SIGNED: *L. Colter* _____ DATE: *20/5/98*

PLEASE COMPLETE THE REVIEW SECTION ABOVE WHEN APPROPRIATE AND

RETURN THIS FORM TO *R. SHORT* (SENCO) BY *24/5/98*

Figure 3.4 Completed proforma for an IEP at stage 2 in a secondary school

Figure 3.4 continued

SECTION 4

1. CURRICULAR NEEDS

(a) Priorities: Literacy – especially reading and spelling

(b) Learning objectives: (1) to improve accuracy and fluency of reading (2) develop spelling accuracy

(c) Criteria for success: (1) improvement in tested reading-age (by 4 mths) (2) improvement in general spelling

(d) Monitoring and review arrangements: (1) SENCO is to monitor reading and review (2) regular monitoring of written work

2. TEACHING ARRANGEMENTS

(a) Strategies and techniques: (1) Withdrawal for 30¾ hr sessions/wk (2) Class texts to be differentiated (SEN support on request)

(b) Equipment and materials: (1) Reading Scheme – Flightpath to Reading Level 2 (2) Blackwell Spelling W'shop + PC spelling

3. NON-CURRICULAR NEEDS

(a) Pastoral care arrangements: N/A

(b) Medical requirements: James should wear glasses for reading / writing

SECTION 5

STAFF ACTION PLAN*

(a) _____

(b) (1) listen to James read each lesson using class text (2) highlight technical terms

(c) _____

(d) (2) check all written work for spelling mistakes

(a) (2) worksheets already differentiated. See SENCO re text.

(b) _____

(a) _____

(b) check James wears his glasses appropriately

Notes

NB. Section 4 is to be completed by the SEN co-ordinator before this plan is circulated.

*Staff identified in section 1 who have a teaching role with the pupil should complete section 5 on receipt of this plan.

the progress made by the child as a result of the implementation of the plan within that teacher's lessons. The proforma is then returned to the SEN co-ordinator by the date requested.

Having gathered all the proformas, the SEN co-ordinator can then review the overall success of the plan and complete the appropriate section on the review of the individual education plan ready for the review meeting. An example of additional pastoral care arrangements necessary might be the need to provide time-out facilities for a child exhibiting behavioural problems. The problem might be a child's inability to control outbursts of temper or aggression towards peers or teachers. The agreement between the school, parents and the child would enable the child to leave the classroom to go to a specified place in order to cool down when confrontation becomes likely. The monitoring might involve the child entering information into a log kept in the time-out facility as well as teacher monitoring. The review and success of the arrangement would involve the frequency of use as logged by those involved with the child. An example of additional medical requirements could be to make appropriate arrangements for a diabetic child to administer insulin injections.

It is important to consider if the curricular priorities, monitoring and recording arrangements affect the child's access to, or entitlement under, the National Curriculum. It may be necessary to seek to modify the National Curriculum programmes of study, levels of attainment or assessment arrangements or to exempt the child from part of the National Curriculum, although this is likely to be an infrequent requirement as a result of the Dearing Reviews.

However, any such arrangements that are necessary must be identified and recorded as well as any alternative programmes of study that are to be implemented. It is also important to record the timescales that are involved for each.

Reviews of Progress

It is expected that the SEN co-ordinator will conduct reviews in consultation with the child's class teacher or form/year tutor. Whenever possible parents should also be present at the review meeting, but regardless of whether this is possible, they should always be invited to contribute to the process and be informed of the outcome (see Chapter Six).

A review of five areas
The review needs to address five areas. These are:

1   *The progress that the child has made within the review period.* This will need to be considered in relation to the criteria for success that have been set.
2   *The effectiveness of the IEP* as a whole in meeting the needs of the child.
3   *The contribution that has been made by the parents* to the provision and its effectiveness. For example, how the child has responded to paired reading at home. This might identify a need to provide additional advice and support for the parents.
4   *Additional or updated information and advice should be received and considered.* For example, the child may have started a course of medication or experienced a change in home circumstances. Additional information might have been received from the social services department.
5   *The future action that is to be taken.*

Four possible outcomes
The review could have four possible outcomes:

1   *The child is no longer in need of special help.* It is possible, in the case of a short-term problem, that the provision made has resolved the difficulties being experienced and the child is able to cope successfully with the normal classroom curriculum. In such cases the child's name should remain on the SEN register until such time as the co-ordinator is satisfied that the child's progress will no longer give cause for concern.
2   *The child returns to stage 1.* Where progress continues to be satisfactory using this planning and review process for at least two review periods, the SEN co-ordinator may decide that the child is no longer in need of specific provision and can return to the provision and monitoring that is used at stage 1.
3   *The child continues to receive help at stage 2.* If the progress of the child has been at least satisfactory as a result of the provision made, then a new IEP can be drawn up using the knowledge and experience gained. New targets can be set in the light of this experience. The length of time between reviews may be gradually extended if progress continues to be satisfactory after at least two review periods. For example, 6-monthly review periods could be extended to coincide with the school's normal procedures for reporting to parents or the statutory requirement to report annually.
4   *The child moves on to stage 3.* Where the child's progress has not been satisfactory for at least two review periods then additional advice and expertise should be sought. This will inevitably come from outside the school and should only be done after discussing the situation in person with the parents.

Where a child's learning experiences have been broken down into small steps of appropriately differentiated work to meet particular needs and difficulties, the child could remain at stage 1 or 2 throughout his or her school career. This would imply that the school has been able to make adequate and appropriate provision that has enabled steady progress to be maintained for a child with special needs without having to make use of specialist support services. A sample proforma for a stage-2 review is presented in the Appendices as A9.

As with the review of help given at stage 1 the only section that can be completed prior to the meeting, apart from the child's details, is the summary of progress made section. This can be completed by the SEN co-ordinator using the information obtained from the proformas that have been returned by the class or subject teachers (see Figures 3.3 and 3.4). The other sections can be completed at the meeting as further information is received. The decisions of the meeting for future action should be recorded as well as the recommendations for the next review period, if appropriate. Where a new IEP is needed, this could be developed at this time saving the need to hold a further meeting. An example of a completed proforma for the review of an individual education plan is presented at Figure 3.5.

The intention of the procedures outlined is to be able to use these proformas in conjunction with one another to move effectively and efficiently through the various stages. Each stage can be developed using the information acquired and recorded from the previous stage. Hence, the review of stage 1 will identify the provision that will be made at stage 2 enabling the co-ordinator to, at least, make a draft of the IEP.

The IEP proforma can be given to each person identified on the circulation list. Where more than one member of the teaching staff have contact with the child, each teacher will need to fill in the staff action plan section that will identify how they will fulfil the needs of the plan. At the end of the allotted time, staff can complete the review section of the form and return it to the SEN co-ordinator who will then collate the information to inform the review of the IEP with the parents. This review will make a decision about future provision which will form the basis of a new IEP, thus beginning the whole cycle again. All these records must be kept as they will be required as evidence should the child progress beyond stage 2.

Summary of Stages 1 and 2 Policy and Practice

Each school is required to have a written policy concerning special educational needs which specifies the principles by which its SEN provision is organised and delivered. Special needs co-ordinators are responsible for the day-to-day operation of that policy. They also have to ensure that the

_____ BELVIEW _____ SCHOOL

REVIEW OF INDIVIDUAL EDUCATION PLAN

STAGE 2: REVIEW NO. ____1____

NAME: James Truggles   FORM: 7MD   DATE OF BIRTH: 15/10/88

DATE OF REVIEW: 4/5/98

PRESENT: R. Short, T. Johnstone, Mr and Mrs L. Truggles, James Truggles

1. SUMMARY OF PROGRESS MADE: James' reading age is now 9 yrs 11 mths — an improvement of 5 mths over the review period and nearing the target. Subject teachers report an improvement in the fluency of his reading and an ability to spell the 'technical' words of their subject. Written work still contains a large number of errors although much of the basic spelling is accurate.

2. VIEWS OF PARENT: Mr & Mrs Truggles are pleased with James' progress in reading. They have regularly listened to him read at home and will continue to do so. Spelling is more of a problem and they are v. concerned.

3. VIEWS OF CHILD: Reading is getting easier. But James does not like coming to D3 for reading. Easier texts in lessons are great but spelling is 'boring'.

4. EFFECTIVENESS OF PLAN: Overall the plan has been effective in improving reading but not so effective with the spelling. Parents' help at home has been valuable and they are willing to continue.

5. UPDATED/ADDITIONAL INFORMATION: _____ James needs to wear his glasses all the time.

6. FUTURE ACTION: (please tick as appropriate)

(a) REVERT TO STAGE 1   [ ]

(b) NEW IEP AT STAGE 2   [✓]

(c) MOVE TO STAGE 3   [ ]

SUPPORT SERVICE(S) TO BE INVOLVED AT STAGE 3 _____

_____

RECOMMENDATIONS FOR NEW IEP: (if appropriate) _____

(1) A similar programme.

(2) Withdraw for reading for 1 session and provide in-class support for the other 2 by agreement with English teacher.

(3) Make IT resources available with spell check for some work.

(4) Provide additional work for parents to use at home.

SIGNED: ___L. Truggles_____ (parent)

___James Truggles_____ (child if appropriate)

___R. SHORT_____ (SEN co-ordinator)

Figure 3.5 Completed proforma for use at a review at stage 2

statutory requirements of the school concerning meeting pupils' needs are fulfilled. A summary of the policy and practice required for schools to meet their obligations at stages 1 and 2 is presented below and in the Appendices as A10.

Does your school have:
- a whole-school policy for record keeping?
- effective means of collecting information – from previous or feeder schools, other services and agencies etc.?
- a range of effective screening procedures?
- an SEN link teacher in each subject department? (secondary schools)
- a whole-school policy for reporting to parents?
- a whole-school policy for identifying and recording progress?
- a suitable, private room for consultation with parents?
- a policy for INSET on SEN for non-specialist staff?
- INSET provision on SEN?

For an individual child has the class/year teacher:
- clearly specified the cause for concern?
- collected the appropriate information?
- collected reports on the child in the school setting from appropriate sources?
- informed the head teacher, the SEN co-ordinator and those with parental responsibility that the child is being considered under stage 1 procedures?
- discussed the situation with those with parental responsibility and sought their views?
- contacted any other agencies or individuals whom those with parental responsibility would like involved?
- sought the views of the child?
- collected information from the child's GP and/or social services and/or educational welfare service as agreed with those with parental responsibility, if appropriate?

Does the INDIVIDUAL EDUCATION PLAN set out:
- the nature of the learning difficulties experienced?
- learning objectives and targets to be achieved?
- the timespan in which to achieve targets?
- the staff to be involved?
- the frequency of any support to be given?
- any specific programmes and/or activities to be used?
- any parental help to be given?
- criteria for success?
- monitoring and recording arrangements?
- the teaching strategies and techniques to be used?
- the equipment and materials to be used?
- any pastoral care arrangements?
- any medical requirements?
- the review date?
- the people to be involved with the review?

Figure 3.6 Checklist on stages 1 and 2 policy and practice

CHAPTER FOUR

Involving Outside Specialists to Help Meet SEN at Stage 3

INTRODUCTION

Consideration of a child for help at stage 3 of the 5-stage model for meeting SEN typically results from dissatisfaction with the child's progress at a meeting held to review the child's IEP at stage 2. If the conclusion of the meeting is that the child is making insufficient progress despite receiving all the help the school can itself provide then the next step is to involve specialist help from outside the school.

While this step will mostly result from a stage-2 review there are occasions when decisions to involve outside specialists will be made for children at stage 1 or even earlier. For example, in the case of a pupil newly arrived at the school whose records, or whose performance on entry tests, indicate that specialist help will be needed, stage 3 procedures would be implemented immediately rather than progressing through stages 1 and 2.

ROLE OF THE SEN CO-ORDINATOR AT STAGE 3

At stage 3 the SEN co-ordinator continues to take lead responsibility for managing the child's special educational provision. Specifically, the SEN co-ordinator's responsibilities at stage 3 include the following.

Collaboration with child's teacher(s)
The SEN co-ordinator will need to continue to liaise closely with the child's

class teacher (primary) or subject teachers and head of year (secondary) in order to design the most appropriate programme for the child. This is important in order to communicate to the child's teacher(s) that involving outside specialists should be seen as strengthening the team of which they are an essential element rather than passing on the responsibility to someone else.

Consultation with head teacher

As always, it is important to keep the head teacher informed about all aspects of provisions for meeting SEN. It is therefore necessary for the SEN co-ordinator to consult with the head when a move to stage 3 and the involvement of outside specialists is being considered.

Informing the LEA

Since LEAs have a duty to identify all children with SEN for whom they are responsible they need to know about all children at stage 3. The Code of Practice recommends that LEAs should write to schools periodically to seek information about pupils who are at stage 3. The SEN co-ordinator will therefore need to have a record of all pupils who are at stage 3 and should inform the LEA when children are added to the list.

Reviewing information on child

The SEN co-ordinator should review all existing records on the child including the information gathered by the school at stages 1 and 2. This is in addition to considering the report of the stage-2 review which triggered the move to stage 3.

Meeting with parents

The SEN co-ordinator should meet with parents to discuss the child's progress in general and the reasons for moving to stage 3 in particular. This discussion would normally take place at the stage-2 review meeting, but if parents were unable to attend this the SEN co-ordinator would need to arrange a meeting with them specifically for this purpose. Parental approval should then be sought for involvement of the specialist(s) considered to be most helpful.

Contacting relevant specialist(s)

The SEN co-ordinator should arrange for the outside specialist whose field is most relevant to the particular child's special needs to come into the school to discuss the child's difficulties and possibly to carry out some form of assessment. In many cases the first specialist to be involved will be the educational psychologist who is assigned to the school. The educational psychologist may decide to work directly with the child or to provide guidance to the child's teachers. Subsequently the SEN co-ordinator and educational psychologist may decide to call in other specialists such as peripatetic teachers or therapists (see later section for the roles of outside specialists likely to be involved with children with SEN in mainstream schools).

When additional specialists are to be involved the SEN co-ordinator will need to keep a record of:

- the further advice that is sought;
- the arrangements made for the child pending the receipt of this additional advice;
- the arrangements made with the specialist already involved for reviewing the situation following the receipt of further advice.

Keeping parents informed
Once the SEN co-ordinator has consulted with the outside specialist(s) then the child' parents should be informed about the likely course of action and invited to participate in revising their child's IEP.

Drawing up an IEP
Following the information and advice received from the various specialists the SEN co-ordinator needs to liaise with parents, teachers and outside specialists in order to draft a new Individual Educational Plan. Ideally, the SEN co-ordinator will organise a meeting of everyone concerned with the child at which the IEP can be agreed. To facilitate this process all participants should be asked to bring along to the meeting information on their up-to-date observations and assessments of the child and on priorities for the child from their perspective. To help parents participate fully in this process the guidelines provided in Chapter Six for facilitating parental involvement in assessments and reviews should be followed.

Final form of the IEP
The final form of the IEP should include:

- the names of everyone involved in designing the IEP;
- the reasons for identifying the child with SEN at stage 3;

- specific curricular priorities;
- specific learning objectives in key curricular areas;
- criteria for evaluating success;
- arrangements for monitoring and review of progress;
- general teaching strategies (e.g. withdrawal or support teaching);
- specific teaching techniques;
- special equipment or materials needed;
- frequency and timing of support provided by outside specialists;
- arrangements for pastoral care;
- arrangements for meeting any medical needs the child has.

Schools will, of course, want to develop their own systems for recording and disseminating information about IEPs. These factors are vitally important in determining the effectiveness of SEN provisions within schools. For example, IEP forms which do not clearly state specific targets and criteria for assessing progress towards these targets will be of little value. However, IEP forms which are time consuming to fill in will engender staff resistance and cause delays. Thus, the actual forms used and the procedures used to communicate with all the people involved with individual children with SEN must be ones which optimise the efficiency of the process. A sample completed proforma for an IEP of a child at stage 3 in a primary school is presented in Figure 4.1. A blank version of this proforma is repeated in the Appendices as A11.

The IEP form (Figure 4.1) will be completed by the SEN co-ordinator, in conjunction with the relevant specialists, in accordance with the decisions made at the meeting. The input that will be provided by the specialists will be specified, as well as the school's input. It will be necessary for class teachers to complete the staff action plan to show how they will incorporate the specialist support or guidance into the normal teaching of the child, in addition to making other appropriate provision from the school's resources. At the end of the IEP form teachers should complete the review section and return it to the SEN co-ordinator in order to inform the review meeting.

In secondary schools the situation is more complex in that instead of one class teacher children typically have several subject teachers. Children also have form teachers who may teach them for one of their subjects and have some pastoral responsibilities along with either a head of year or head of house. Therefore, in secondary schools, although the IEP process will be similar to that described above, more people will be involved which makes co-ordination more difficult. The procedure for completing an IEP form and for disseminating the finished IEP are therefore different to that in primary schools which means that a slightly different IEP form and procedure are needed for secondary schools. A sample completed proforma for an IEP of a child at stage 3 in a secondary school is presented in Figure 4.2. A blank version of this proforma is repeated in the Appendices as A12. The same

WONDER ROAD _____ SCHOOL

INDIVIDUAL EDUCATION PLAN
STAGE 3

SECTION 1
NAME: _ALICE TRUGGLES_ FORM: _2Y_ DATE OF BIRTH: _27 / 2 / 87_
DATE OF PLAN: _4/3/94_ REVIEW DATE: _21/7/94_
SUPPORT SERVICE(S) INVOLVED _HEARING IMPAIRED SERVICE_
CONTACT PERSON(S) _MRS B. LIVELY_ TEL. _761343_
_____ TEL. _____

CIRCULATION*: PARENTS, SUPPORT SERVICE(S), HEAD, <u>CLASS TEACHER</u>, OTHERS
MRS C. BROWN (HEAD DINNER SUPERVISOR)

PEOPLE TO BE INVOLVED IN THE REVIEW: PARENTS, SEN CO-ORDINATOR, SUPPORT
SERVICE CONTACT(S), CLASS TEACHER, OTHERS
_____

SECTION 2
REASONS FOR IDENTIFICATION: _Alice has glue ear condition in both ears. She is due for an operation to fit grommets in the near future. Hearing Impaired Service also identify a monoaural hearing loss of high frequency sounds in her right ear._

SECTION 3
REVIEW (including progress made with evidence where appropriate):
(a) School _Alice has made slow progress. Even though new words have been emphasised Alice's vocabulary has developed slowly. Some words are still mispronounced. Alice also finds difficulty in following verbal instructions. She seems to miss quite a lot of verbal messages and instructions._
(b) Support service _____

RECOMMENDATIONS FOR FUTURE ACTION:
(a) School _Alice should be kept at Stage 3. Perhaps some form of instruction in lip-reading might help. Also the insertion of grommets may improve her hearing. She needs more small group work with less distraction from background noise._
(b) Support service _____

SIGNED: _Caroline Davis (Class Teacher)_ DATE: _13/7/94_

PLEASE RETURN TO _Mrs J. White_ (SENCO) BY _14/7/94_

Figure 4.1 Completed proforma for an IEP at stage 3 in a primary school

SECTION 4	SECTION 5
1. CURRICULAR NEEDS	STAFF ACTION PLAN*
(a) Priorities: *Communication*	(a)
(b) Learning objectives: *to ensure that Alice learns new words correctly to develop her vocabulary*	(b) *Ensure clear diction and slow delivery Emphasise/repeat new words*
(c) Criteria for success: *correct pronunciation of words*	(c) *Listen to Alice speak and read aloud*
(d) Monitoring and review arrangements: *(i) Daily (ii) Mrs Linely (H/S) will visit Alice on a weekly basis*	(d) *Daily*
2. TEACHING ARRANGEMENTS	
(a) Strategies and techniques: *(i) Alice to sit at right-hand side of classroom (ii) Teacher must face Alice when speaking*	(a) ✓ ✓
(b) Equipment and materials: *N/A*	(b)
3. NON-CURRICULAR NEEDS	
(a) Pastoral care arrangements: *N/A*	(a)
(b) Medical requirements: *Ear drops - to be administered at home before school*	(b)

Notes
NB. Section 4 is to be completed by the SEN co-ordinator before being circulated.

*Staff identified in section 1 who have a teaching role with the pupil should complete section 5 on receipt of this plan.

BELVIEW SCHOOL

INDIVIDUAL EDUCATION PLAN
STAGE 3

SECTION 1

NAME: _Alice Truggles_   FORM: _7RD_   DATE OF BIRTH: _27_/_2_/_87_

DATE OF PLAN: _1/10/98_   REVIEW DATE: _23/3/99_

SUPPORT SERVICE(S) INVOLVED _Hearing impaired Service, Speech Therapy_

CONTACT PERSON(S) _Mrs B Lively_   TEL. _761343_
Mrs H Reason   TEL. _766475_

CIRCULATION*: PARENTS, SUPPORT SERVICE(S), HEAD, SEN CO-ORDINATOR, HEAD OF YEAR, FORM TUTOR, SUBJECT STAFF

_AB, DA, FH, FE, HM, JN, LE, PN, RO, SM, TA._

PEOPLE TO BE INVOLVED IN THE REVIEW: PARENTS, SEN CO-ORDINATOR, SUPPORT SERVICE CONTACT(S), OTHERS

SECTION 2

REASONS FOR IDENTIFICATION: _Alice has a neural hearing loss of high frequency sounds in her right ear. She currently has grommets fitted to both ears._

SECTION 3

REVIEW (including progress made with evidence where appropriate):

(a) School _ALICE HAS MADE STEADY PROGRESS WITH HER SCIENCE. THE SUPPORT IN PRACTICAL SESSIONS HAS BEEN INVALUABLE. SHE SEEMS TO HAVE GRASPED THE CONCEPTS PRESENTED, LEARNED THE CORRECT PRONUNCIATION OF TECHNICAL TERMS. CONTRIBUTION TO CLASS DISCUSSIONS HAS BEEN LIMITED. WORKED WELL IN SMALL GROUPS_

(b) Support service _____

RECOMMENDATIONS FOR FUTURE ACTION:

(a) School _CONTINUED SUPPORT REQUESTED FOR PRACTICAL LESSONS_

(b) Support service _____

SIGNED: _J Smith._   DATE: _10/3/_

PLEASE RETURN TO _R. SHORT_   (SENCO)   BY _16/3/99_

Figure 4.2 Completed proforma for an IEP at stage 3 in a secondary school

SECTION 4

1. CURRICULAR NEEDS

(a) Priorities: *Communication*

(b) Learning objectives: *to develop*
(1) *vocabulary & correct pronunciation*
(2) *accurate verbal communication*

(c) Criteria for success: *Involvement with class discussion & understanding verbal instructions*

(d) Monitoring and review arrangements: *Lesson by lesson*

2. TEACHING ARRANGEMENTS

(a) Strategies and techniques: (1) *Alice to sit at r/h side of class* (2) *Teacher to face class when speaking* (3) *Small group work when possible*

(b) Equipment and materials: *N/A H.I.S support for ½hr per week School / support staff available on request.*

3. NON-CURRICULAR NEEDS

(a) Pastoral care arrangements: *N/A*

(b) Medical requirements: *N/A.*

SECTION 5

STAFF ACTION PLAN*

(a)

(b) *EMPHASISE*

(c) *CHECK INDIVIDUALLY WITH ALICE*

(d)

(a) (1) ✓
(2) ✓
(3) *WORK CAN BE ARRANGED IN THIS WAY*

(b) *SUPPORT REQUESTED FOR PRACTICAL WORK.*

(a)

(b)

Notes
NB. Section 4 is to be completed by the SEN co-ordinator before being circulated.

*Staff identified in section 1 who have a teaching role with the pupil should complete section 5 on receipt of this plan.

procedure used for completion of the secondary IEP form (Figure 4.2) will apply as for the primary IEP form with the exception that every member of staff who teaches the child will need to complete the staff action plan.

Arranging a Review

When the IEP is being drafted the SEN co-ordinator is responsible for setting a date on which the child's progress will be reviewed. Reviews should ideally be conducted once a term. Reminders of the date, time and place set for review meetings may need to be given a few days before the meeting. Reviews should be organised at times when it is possible for outside specialists and parents to attend. Everyone who is concerned with the child, including the parents, should be invited to attend the review meeting. All participants should be asked to bring along to the meeting information on their up-to-date observations and assessments of the child relevant to the targets set for their involvement with the child. They should also have prepared tentative future priorities for the child from their perspective. To help parents participate fully in this process the guidelines provided in Chapter Seven for facilitating parental involvement in assessments and reviews should be followed.

Conducting a Review

The SEN co-ordinator should normally chair review meetings which will need to focus on the following:

- progress which the child has made towards each of the targets set;
- effectiveness of the IEP in ensuring the child's needs are being met;
- possible need for further specialist assessment and advice;
- updated assessment information necessary to revise targets;
- revision of IEP, especially setting of new targets;
- future action, including likelihood of need for referral for statutory assessment.

A sample completed proforma for the review of an IEP at stage 3 is presented in Figure 4.3. A blank version of this proforma is repeated in the Appendices as A13. The purpose of the review form (Figure 4.3) is to summarise the information received from everyone concerned with the child while the IEP has been in operation. This will then provide the basis for discussions about progress made, including identification of strategies which have been successful. In this way it will facilitate decision making about future provision. It may then be possible to draft a new IEP at the review meeting negating the need to hold a separate meeting for this purpose.

WONDER ROAD _____ SCHOOL

REVIEW OF INDIVIDUAL EDUCATION PLAN

STAGE 3: REVIEW NO. ___1___

SECTION 1

NAME: _ALICE TRUGGLES_ FORM: __24__ DATE OF BIRTH: _27_ / _2_ / _87_

DATE OF REVIEW: _21_ / _7_ / _94_

PRESENT: _Mr & Mrs TRUGGLES, ALICE TRUGGLES, MRS B. LIVELY (HIS), MRS T. WHITE (SENO)_
MRS C. DAVIS (CLASS TEACHER)

SECTION 2

1. SUMMARY OF PROGRESS MADE:

   (a) School: _Alice has made slow progress. Her vocabulary is not developing at an appropriate rate for her age. Instructions and discussions present problems as Alice appears to miss parts of what is said. Some words are mispronounced._

   (b) Support service: _Although Alice is sitting in the correct position in the classroom and watching the teacher, she still does not hear fully what is said. Her condition is deteriorating as is shown by her latest audiometry test results._

2. VIEWS OF PARENT: _Mr and Mrs Truggles have also noticed that Alice is having difficulty following what they say. Classroom seating position has helped and they also make sure that they face Alice when speaking to her._

3. VIEWS OF CHILD: _Alice finds the background noise of the classroom a problem when working or listening to others._

4. EFFECTIVENESS OF PLAN: _The plan has only had limited effect. The position of Alice in the classroom and the need to face people when they are speaking to her has helped. Alice needs more small group work to help develop vocabulary and correct pronunciation._

5. UPDATED/ADDITIONAL INFORMATION: _Alice is having grommets fitted over the summer holiday._

SECTION 3

6. FUTURE ACTION: (please tick as appropriate)

   (a) Revert to stage 2 ☐

   (b) New IEP at stage 2 ☐   Stage 3 ☑

   (c)(i) Support service(s) to be involved: _HEARING IMPAIRED SERVICE_

   (d) Move to stage 4 ☐

RECOMMENDATIONS FOR NEW IEP: _(1) Similar classroom arrangements_
(2) Individual work with HIS to develop: lip-reading skills; vocabulary; pronunciation.
(3) Development of more small group teaching / working arrangements

NB(1) Contact Health Authority concerning Speech Therapy input
(2) Monitor arrangements regarding the effectiveness of grommets

SIGNED: _E. Truggles_ _____ (parent)

Alice Truggles _____ (child if appropriate)

B. Lively _____ (support service)

_____ (support service)

T. White _____ (SEN co-ordinator)

Figure 4.3 Completed proforma for use at a review at stage 3

Considering Future Options

A key function of review meetings is to consider the most appropriate options for ensuring that the child's SEN will continue to be met. There are three main options: (1) the child continues to be supported at stage 3; (2) the child's level of support reverts to stage 2; (3) the child is referred to the LEA for statutory assessment. These three options are discussed below.

1 *Continue at stage 3.* If the child is making satisfactory progress then it will probably be decided to continue at stage 3. This will involve revising the child's IEP and arranging for a further review, as discussed above. If, at the second review, the child's progress continues to be satisfactory then the SEN co-ordinator should consult with the head teacher and outside specialists about increasing the review period, perhaps to half yearly or yearly.

2 *Revert to stage 2.* If the child has made excellent progress over two consecutive review periods then the SEN co-ordinator should discuss with the head teacher and specialists involved whether the child continues to need specialist support at stage 3. It may then be decided that the child's SEN can be met at stage 2 or even stage 1. The child would then be listed as being supported at stage 1 or 2 and action appropriate to the relevant stage would be taken.

3 *Referral for statutory assessment.* If the child is not making satisfactory progress by the time of the second review then the SEN co-ordinator should consult with the specialists involved and the head teacher about the possibility of requesting the LEA to conduct a statutory assessment in order to consider preparing a statement of the child's special educational needs.

An approach to the LEA for a statutory assessment to be conducted must be endorsed by the person at the school who has overall responsibility for SEN provision at the school (the 'responsible person'). In most cases this will be the head teacher or chair of the governing body or the governor designated to take responsibility for SEN provision in the school.

Since most children will have moved through stages 1 to 3 over a period of time the school will have available considerable written evidence to support a request for a statutory assessment.

On record will be
- results of educational assessments conducted at the school;
- IEPs developed for the child at stages 2 and 3;
- reports of IEP review meetings;

- information from the specialists involved at stage 3;
- possibly information from health and social service involvement;
- views of the parents and, where appropriate, views of the child.

Also, since in most cases the LEA's educational psychologist and in many cases LEA support service staff will have been involved with the child at stage 3, the LEA should be able to decide quickly whether to conduct a statutory assessment. If it is decided to conduct an assessment then the school will be able to use the written information referred to above to help them prepare their contribution to the assessment process.

BACKGROUND AND ROLE OF OUTSIDE SPECIALISTS

There are a wide range of outside specialists whose role encompasses work with children who have SEN. It is important for SEN co-ordinators to be knowledgeable about these specialists and the kind of help they can provide. The backgrounds and roles of those specialists who are likely to be involved with children with SEN in mainstream schools are outlined below.

Educational psychologists

Educational psychologists are experienced teachers who have undertaken professional training in educational psychology. They have a role with the whole range of special needs including children with learning and behavioural difficulties as well as those with sensory losses and chronic illnesses. They may work directly with a child or provide guidance to teachers or parents. Part of their role is to submit psychological advice for statutory assessments at stage 4.

Advisers/Inspectors for SEN

Advisers and inspectors for SEN are typically experienced teachers who have also had senior management experience in either a mainstream or special school. Their responsibilities include developing and disseminating LEA policy on SEN, providing specialist advice to schools on provision for children with SEN and monitoring the quality of SEN provision in schools as members of OFSTED teams. However, they are also a potential source of advice regarding the SEN of individual pupils.

Advisory teachers
Advisory teachers are experienced teachers who have typically developed expertise in a particular aspect of education. They are employed by many LEAs to work under the guidance of specific advisers. The role of advisory teachers for SEN tends to focus on providing advice and support to teachers on meeting the SEN of a number of pupils. The role of advisory teachers for information technology encompasses the provision of guidance and training of teachers of children with SEN in information technology.

Peripatetic learning support teachers
Most LEAs have services with names such as 'learning support service' or 'language and learning service'. They are staffed by teachers experienced in working with children with learning difficulties. Their role typically involves teaching individual or small groups of children who have literacy or numeracy difficulties in several schools on a small number of occasions each week. Alternatively they can provide guidance to teachers in designing programmes for such children which will be taught by school staff. In some LEAs such learning support teachers are part of a generic support service which includes teachers of children with hearing impairment, visual impairment and behavioural difficulties. But in the majority of LEAs separate support services are provided for each area of specialism, as described below.

Peripatetic specialists for hearing impaired children
Most LEAs have services for hearing impaired children which are staffed by qualified teachers of the deaf. They work with children with all levels of hearing impairment in special schools, units in mainstream schools and those in ordinary classes. They assess and monitor children's hearing, provide supervision in the use of hearing aids, carry out diagnostic testing and are also available to provide counselling and careers guidance when required (Hegarty, 1993). They do not teach children directly but provide guidance on teaching strategies and help to monitor children's progress. They also provide access to further specialists in the field of hearing impairment such as audiologists and ear, nose and throat surgeons.

Peripatetic specialists for visually impaired children
Many LEAs have services for children with visual impairment which are staffed by qualified teachers of visually impaired children. Because blindness and poor vision are such low-incidence impairments (in the UK) smaller LEAs may not have a service, others will have only one or two staff who may be integrated into a sensory impairment service along with teachers of

children with hearing impairment. These teachers work with children who are blind as well as those who are often termed partially sighted (low vision). They provide guidance to teachers regarding the management of different types of visual impairment, the assessment of children's progress and on appropriate teaching strategies. They tend not to teach children directly but to provide guidance on the use of visual aids and on the development of social skills as well as being available to counsel children who need such help (Hegarty, 1993). They also provide access to other professionals in the field of visual impairment, such as optometrists, ophthalmologists and orientation and mobility specialists.

Behavioural support service teachers

Teachers working for the behavioural support service have typically had experience with children who exhibit emotional or behavioural problems in special schools or units. Their role involves providing guidance and support for mainstream teachers in coping with children with behavioural problems. They do not usually work directly with the child but help teachers to implement behavioural management programmes and differentiate curriculum content.

Education officers for SEN

LEAs typically have an Education Officer (EO) and a number of Assistant Education Officers (AEOs) who have particular responsibility for children with SEN. Their overall role is to ensure that provisions for children with SEN follow LEA policy and are well organised. Within this role there are several specific tasks including administration of the statutory assessment and statementing process and oversight of financial delegation to schools of money earmarked for SEN provision. However, LEAs differ in the ways they allocate tasks to EOs and AEOs and in their organisation of many aspects of the administration procedures established for SEN. It is therefore important for SEN co-ordinators to find out how things are organised in their LEA and thereby establish what information and advice they can expect from each EO and AEO.

Education welfare officers

Education Welfare Officers (EWOs) are employed by LEAs to provide a link between home and school. EWOs typically have either a teaching or social work background. They are often based in a secondary school but have responsibility for a cluster of schools. They can be of help to SEN co-ordinators by visiting children's parents to investigate absences or to discuss difficulties which children are encountering or creating at school.

Social workers

Social workers employed by social services come from a variety of back-gounds. An increasing number have completed qualifications in social work, many have social science degrees, others have neither degrees nor training but have gained considerable experience in social services. Part of the job of social workers is to work with families who have children with special needs. Parents of children with moderate and severe levels of special needs should have a social worker assigned to them who they can contact for information about such things as the benefits available to them and respite care. In some cases social workers may be involved in contributing to statutory assessments at stage 4, particularly where their knowledge of a child's home circum-stances is relevant. They may also be able to provide valuable information about a child's family background to SEN co-ordinators at stage 3.

Careers officers

Some careers services have specialist officers for advising young people with special needs about training opportunities and job options. However, this is not available in all parts of the country and it is unlikely that such officers will be familiar with the vocational needs associated with all types of disabilities. The careers service is, however, a potential source of guidance for teachers in helping young people with special needs consider employment possibilities and the wide diversity of training opportunities available to them after they turn 16.

School medical officers

School medical officers are qualified doctors who are employed by health authorities to provide medical guidance to schools. Their role is not to provide treatment but to assess children's physical health and development and identify any problems so that children can be referred to the appropriate specialist. They therefore provide a link to other medical personnel such as family doctors, paediatricians and psychiatrists, as well as being a source of referral for other health service workers such as speech therapists, physio-therapists and occupational therapists. In addition, part of their role is to submit medical advice for statutory assessments at stage 4.

Community nursing service

The community nursing service is staffed by qualified nurses employed by health authorities. The service is available to schools to deal with any medical or related problems which children are experiencing. For example, they can provide sex education lessons for children with SEN and help girls with learning difficulties to cope with menstruation. They can also provide guidance or assistance for pupils with the chronic health problems associated with such conditions as spina bifida and asthma.

Speech and language therapists

Speech and language therapists are employed by health authorities rather than LEAs. Because of the shortage of therapists it is often difficult to gain access to sufficient speech therapy time to cater for children with SEN in mainstream schools. Speech therapy training courses prepare therapists to work with both adults and children. With children, the speech therapist's role is much broader than simply focusing on speech difficulties such as articulation problems. Help can also be provided to children with delayed language development as well as to those who have problems with fluency (stammers) and those with voice problems such as hoarseness, in addition to those children with physical disabilities who have feeding problems. Speech therapists may work directly with a child (usually in their clinics) or may assess children and then provide guidance to teachers and parents, including exercises designed to remediate the child's difficulties. They are also a source of general advice for teachers on dealing with speech and language difficulties encountered in schools. Access to speech therapy can be gained through referral by the child's family doctor in addition to through links between LEAs and health authorities.

Occupational therapists

Occupational therapists are also employed by health authorities and are trained to work with children and adults in a wide variety of settings. One area in which they are particularly helpful is providing guidance for teachers of children with visual perceptual difficulties. Such problems are often encountered by children with specific learning difficulties and those with cerebral palsy. Another area in which they provide assistance is with children who have physical disabilities who need special equipment or techniques to help them with dressing or toileting. Access to occupational therapy can be gained through referral by the child's family doctor.

Physiotherapists

Physiotherapists are also mostly employed by health authorities and mainly work with adult clients in hospital settings. However, some physiotherapists specialise in working with children. These paediatric physiotherapists are generally employed in special schools for children with physical disabilities. They work directly with children, assessing their difficulties and then providing treatment. They also help teachers with such things as working out the most comfortable positions for children to adopt in classrooms. In addition, they provide a link to other specialists such as orthopaedic surgeons. Access to physiotherapy can be gained through referral by the child's family doctor or by contacting a special school for children with physical disabilities.

Voluntary agency staff

The numerous voluntary agencies which operate in the field of disability are a potential source of specialists who can provide information and advice which is helpful in developing IEPs. For example, a social worker employed by MENCAP can contribute knowledge of local recreational facilities for children with learning difficulties. Alternatively, a field officer employed by the RNIB can provide information on aids and materials which may be of help to teachers in planning programmes. Access to the staff of voluntary agencies is by various means including: newspaper helpline columns; local councils for voluntary services; and the Citizens' Advice Bureaux.

STRATEGIES FOR MAKING MOST EFFECTIVE USE OF OUTSIDE SPECIALISTS

An important aspect of the SEN co-ordinator's role at stage 3 is liaising with the various outside specialists (listed above) who can provide information and guidance regarding individual children or advice on overall provision for SEN within the school. It is therefore essential that SEN co-ordinators develop effective working relationships with a network of specialists who can be of assistance to the school. Establishing such relationships will ensure the most efficient use of specialist time and expertise and therefore optimise the benefit to the school as well as increasing the satisfaction of the specialists themselves. Specialists understandably prefer to work in schools where they are appreciated and their expertise is efficiently used. So the more effective the working relationship, the more willing the specialist will be to return to the school.

Developing a Network

The first step is for SEN co-ordinators to make sure that they are aware of and know how to contact all of the outside specialists who could possibly be of help to the school. The above list of specialists can be used as an initial checklist which can be added to by various means. First, as mentioned above, the listed specialists can provide access to others who may be useful resources in particular cases. Second, talking with SEN co-ordinators in nearby schools can reveal additional specialists who operate in the local community and who have been found useful. Third, parents may be a source of knowledge of specialists who have been of help to their children. A14 in the Appendices provides a checklist of the outside specialists whose roles have been discussed in this chapter along with other agencies and parent support organisations. Space is provided for the names, addresses and telephone numbers of local contacts to be written in. Also in the Appendices (A19) is a list of addresses of national organisations for children with SEN and their parents, plus a space to write in local contact details.

Establishing Rapport

It is important for SEN co-ordinators to establish a rapport with each of the outside specialists who comes into the school. They should be made to feel welcome in the school and made to feel that their contribution is appreciated. The first time they come into the school a point should be made of introducing them to the head teacher or member of the management team who has responsibility for SEN. Specialists should be asked about what they need in order to do their job within the school. For example, do they need a quiet room in order to assess children or would they rather work with children in their classrooms?

SEN co-ordinators should use the skills discussed in Chapter Eight in order to develop effective working relationships with specialists. For example, listening skills can be used to find out each specialist's needs and assertion skills can be used to ensure that they are provided with what they need to carry out their job effectively within the school. Also, problem-solving skills can be used to resolve any differences of opinion which occur between specialists and school staff.

Finding Out Interests

When rapport has been developed with specialists it is valuable to engage them in conversation in order to find out about their experience and interests relevant to children with SEN. Listening skills can be used to explore specialists' particular strengths or interests within the SEN field. For example, some educational psychologists are particularly interested and experienced in counselling approaches while others have behavioural modification as their speciality. Once such interests are known then the SEN co-ordinator can consider ways in which they can be put to use within the school, perhaps by means of the specialist providing in-service training for the staff. This has a double pay-off in that it raises the status of special needs within the school and increases the credibility of specialists in the eyes of staff. Also, following acknowledgement of their strengths, specialists are likely to be more willing to admit to possible areas of weakness and discuss strategies for bringing other expertise to bear on these.

Efficient Use of Time

It is useful for SEN co-ordinators to find out how specialists prefer to work within the school and then make arrangements to accommodate their requirements as far as possible. Most specialists prefer to make regular visits to the school rather than be called in to face crisis situations. So it may be useful for SEN co-ordinators to discuss this with each specialist to see whether a schedule of visits can be arranged, even if this is only once a term or once a year. If dates are agreed well ahead of the visits then the SEN co-ordinator can organise efficiently for each visit. Before a visit it is usually best to prepare a prioritised list of pupils which specialists are asked to discuss and perhaps observe or assess. Relevant records on these pupils should be brought out so that they are immediately available to the specialist on arrival at the school. An appropriate room should be available for the specialist's use and procedures for getting pupils from their classrooms to the room quickly when they are needed, or for leading specialists to classrooms, should be in place.

Methods of Contact

Many of the specialists who work in the field of SEN spend a large proportion of their time away from their office or clinic and can be difficult to contact. It is therefore important to find out the most effective means of contacting each individual specialist and to make a note of this next to their address book entries. For example, many specialists are out in schools for most of the day but return to their office between 4 p.m. and 5 p.m. Others may call in to their office between 8 a.m. and 9 a.m. each morning. Still others may have one day a week which they spend in their clinic to do paperwork and make phone calls. Finding out these patterns can be very helpful in knowing when are good times for contacting specialists.

Like SEN co-ordinators, many specialists in the SEN field have jobs in which the demands far outstrip the time they have available. In this situation there is a tendency to 'oil the squeaky wheel'. So it is important for SEN co-ordinators to be assertive about contacting specialists. If they are not in the office to receive a call, or are in a meeting, a message should be left for them to return the call as soon as possible. If this does not happen within two days then it is important to call again and repeat the message. Most specialists prefer contact by telephone as this allows more efficient use of their time than letters or meetings but there are times when these alternative forms of contact are more appropriate.

SUMMARY AND CONCLUSIONS

The role of the SEN co-ordinator at stage 3 involves collaborating with school staff, parents and outside specialists as well as developing effective procedures for producing IEPs and reviewing progress. The SEN co-ordinator therefore needs to be aware of the background and role of all the outside specialists who could be of use to schools. Information on a wide range of specialists has been provided and suggestions about how they can be used most effectively were presented. When the school does all it can at stage 3 but children fail to make satisfactory progress then it is necessary to move to stages 4 and perhaps 5, which are discussed in the following chapter.

CHAPTER FIVE

Assessment and Statementing Procedures at Stages 4 and 5

INTRODUCTION

Although it must be realised that stages 4 and 5 are within the control of the local education authority, it is imperative that teachers in general and the SEN co-ordinator in particular understand the procedures and processes involved as well as their responsibilities within stages 4 and 5. The focus of stage 4 is the statutory assessment of children with SEN, which requires that LEAs will work co-operatively with schools, parents and other agencies, first to determine whether a statutory assessment is necessary, and secondly to complete such an assessment.

It is possible that a statutory assessment may be able to highlight ways in which a school can meet the child's needs, perhaps by the provision of a piece of equipment, so that a statement will not be written, though this should have been realised at stage 3. For example, the statutory assessment may reveal some information which was overlooked or not available earlier, which will influence the judgement of the LEA. However, the LEA will normally wish to determine the provision themselves and issue a statement to that effect. Although a statutory assessment may not always lead to the provision of a statement, it must be understood that a statement cannot be written unless a statutory assessment has been undertaken.

Referral to stage 4 may be made by schools or parents. The Code of Practice anticipates this by outlining the responses to these two methods of referral.

REFERRAL FROM THE SCHOOL

The normal course of action would be to refer a child to the LEA after stages 1 to 3 had failed to produce the required result. It should be noted that it will only be possible to request a statutory assessment without having attempted stages 1 to 3 where there are extreme circumstances such as an accident or sudden change in a child's condition, or a new admission to the school from another area.

Referral Following Stages 1 to 3

If the referral follows stages 1 to 3 the evidence needed would include:

1   records to illustrate the chronological picture from the point of identification to the present (assessment, support strategies, discussions with parents and pupils, at stages 1, 2 and 3);
2   evidence of health checks and medical advice;
3   written individual education plans from stages 2 and 3 and evidence of teaching methods used, monitoring arrangements and outcomes;
4   reviews of progress at stages 1, 2 and 3 indicating decisions and results;
5   evidence of the involvement and views of other agencies who have been consulted.

This weight of evidence is needed to assist the LEA to determine that a statutory assessment is the appropriate next step to take.

REFERRAL FROM PARENTS

Should the referral be initiated by the parents, then the LEA must undertake a statutory assessment unless: (1) they have undertaken such an assessment within the last 6 months; or (2) they conclude after further investigation that such an assessment is not necessary.

Action by LEA Following a Request by Parents

Where an LEA receives such a request they should:

1   contact the parents immediately to investigate their concern;
2   ascertain the degree of their involvement with the provision being made for their child;

3 give them full details of the assessment and statementing processes to be undertaken, both orally and in writing, and provide a named LEA officer to contact;
4 write to social services, the health authority and the head teacher of the child's school to inform them that a request has been received from the parents and indicate the help they will need if they decide to undertake an assessment;
5 inform other agencies, such as the educational psychology service, who might later be asked for advice.

ACTION FOLLOWING REFERRAL FROM A SCHOOL

The LEA must serve a notice to the parents that they propose to make an assessment. This notice must explain to the parents the procedure which will be followed, the name of the officer from whom further information may be obtained and indicate their right to make representation and submit written evidence within 29 days.

Steps the LEA Must Take

The LEA must:

1 encourage the parents to make such representation and offer support;
2 refer parents to sources of independent help and information such as support groups and voluntary organisations;
3 ask parents whom they would wish the LEA to consult, other than those agencies which will usually be consulted;
4 give parents written information about the full range of SEN provision available in mainstream and special schools within the LEA;
5 set out clearly the procedures which they will follow and the timescale (see below);
6 explain about the role of the named person, who is independent of the LEA, who can help them through the statementing process.

This information should be given to parents in such a way that the parents do not feel intimidated but are encouraged to participate in the assessment process (see Chapter Six).

TIMESCALES FOR ACTION

The first task of the LEA is to determine whether an assessment should be made. So, within 6 weeks of the date on which they: *either* serve notice to a parent of a proposed assessment, *or* receive a letter from a parent requesting an assessment, they must tell the parent whether they will make an assessment or not. The timescale is as follows:

- *Decision 1 (assessment or not).* If an assessment is being made it must be completed within 10 weeks and then a decision made as to whether to write a statement.
- *Decision 2 (statement or not).* Within 2 weeks of this decision being made it must be communicated to parents *either* by providing a copy of the proposed statement *or* by providing a draft statement *or* by giving notice of the decision not to make a statement, stating the reasons for this.
- *Draft statement.* Within 8 weeks of serving a draft statement the statement should be finalised and sent to parents, school and those agencies which have contributed to the assessment.
- *Final action = 26 weeks = 6 months from the initial request or notice to parent.*

CRITERIA FOR DECIDING TO MAKE A STATUTORY ASSESSMENT

According to the Code, the most critical question the LEA will have to address in deciding whether or not to undertake a statutory assessment is 'whether there is *convincing evidence* that, despite the school, with the help of external specialists, taking relevant and purposeful action to meet the child's learning difficulties, those difficulties remain or have not been remedied sufficiently and may require the LEA to determine the child's special educational provision' (DfE, 1994, p. 52).

In reaching such a decision LEAs will need to see a wide range of evidence from a variety of sources, which may vary according to the special needs of the child.

Evidence to be Provided by Schools

Schools will be asked to provide evidence of:

- their assessment of the child's learning difficulties;
- the action they have taken to address those difficulties;

- the child's academic attainments;
- results of any academic tests including National Curriculum tests (if available) or the teachers' own tests;
- the child's ongoing work, to illustrate progress (or lack of it).

Extent of the Child's Special Needs

LEAs will want evidence of anything that indicates the severity or complexity of the child's special needs. For example, they may wish to note any *significant discrepancies between* the following attainments:

- The child's attainments in National Curriculum (NC) core subjects *and* the attainment of the majority of the child's age peers. That is, a child whose attainments in English, mathematics and science are well below the average for his or her age.
- The child's attainments in NC core subjects *and* the performance expected by the child's teachers, parents or others who have assessed or observed the child, such as an educational psychologist, supported by standardised test data. An example would be a child who performs well orally and has been assessed by an educational psychologist as having at least average intellectual ability and whose attainments in NC core subjects are below average.
- The child's attainments *within* one core subject of the National Curriculum, for example a child whose speaking and listening skills are well above his or her attainments in reading, writing and spelling. Or another child, whose attainments in spelling are well below his or her attainments in other aspects of English.
- The child's attainment in one NC core subject *and* another. For example, a child whose attainments in mathematics are well below his or her attainments in English and/or science.

Further Evidence

LEAs will seek evidence on issues such as:

- the child's health, and any related problems, which may have prevented the child from having participated in a broad, balanced curriculum;
- possible sensory impairments such as a fluctuating hearing loss;
- difficulties with speech or language, such as articulation problems or delayed language development;
- poor school attendance either related to ill-health or other reasons;

- difficulties in the child's family or other home circumstances;
- any emotional and/or behavioural difficulties exhibited by the child.

The LEA's deliberations will always seek to determine whether a school has:

- identified the child's learning difficulties and taken appropriate action at stage 1;
- carefully formulated and regularly monitored individual education plans at stage 2;
- sought and acted upon appropriate advice from other agencies at stage 3;
- worked closely with and taken account of the views of parents throughout;
- sought to provide access to information technology;
- implemented its policies on pastoral care; and
- sought the assistance of medical and social services as and when appropriate.

The SEN co-ordinator should ask, 'Does the evidence I am submitting paint the picture I am attempting to portray?' If the evidence has gaps, the LEA will find them and this may delay the assessment process and the implementation of any subsequent statement.

LEAs will seek particular information for each type of special educational need. For example, for children with specific learning difficulties, they will ask whether evidence can be provided for the discrepancy between apparent potential and performance. The following pages can be used as checklists for the key information required for various special educational needs encountered.

Children with Learning Difficulties

1 Can you demonstrate in what ways the child is not benefiting from working on National Curriculum programmes of study relevant to the appropriate key stage?
2 Can you demonstrate that the National Curriculum core subject level on which the child is working is well below that of his or her peers, and state what you have done to provide him or her with successful learning experiences?
3 Can you provide evidence that the child is falling behind his or her peers in any core subjects, by producing samples of work, records of action, assessments undertaken, standardised tests results?
4 Can you explain how the child's development is at odds with his or her peers, for example immaturity, restricted activities, lack of awareness, little imagination etc.?

Children with Specific Learning Difficulties

1   Can you demonstrate the discrepancies between attainments in the same or different core National Curriculum subjects? Is the child performing better in some aspect of the subject, for example speaking and listening, than in reading and writing?
2   Can you show how the child's performance is incompatible with his or her apparent potential and can you provide detailed evidence to support this? For example, discrepancies between academic attainments and intellectual ability as measured by standardised tests.
3   Have you any standardised test scores which will support your view? For example, results of tests of reading, spelling, mathematics and cognitive ability.
4   Have you clear recorded evidence of the child's strengths and weaknesses particularly in areas of sequencing, auditory or visual perception, memory or language use?
5   Can you provide evidence of the activities which the child has undertaken, the difficulties experienced and the success he or she has had?

Children with Emotional and Behavioural Difficulties

1   Can you provide detailed, dated accounts of the unacceptable behaviours exhibited by the pupil together with any action taken and the outcome of those actions?
2   Is there a significant discrepancy between the child's estimated ability and his or her performance?
3   Is the child withdrawn, lacking in confidence or unable to make and sustain meaningful relationships?
4   Does the child exhibit bizarre, unpredictable, obsessive or disruptive behaviour?
5   Can you provide evidence to show how the child's behaviour is affecting his or her work and/or the work of others in the class?

Children with Physical Disabilities

1   Can you show how the child's disabilities prevent or hinder the child's access to a broad, balanced curriculum?
2   Can you show how the child's needs prevent progress through the levels of the National Curriculum?
3   Does the child have significant self-help difficulties? For example, in feeding, toileting or dressing.

4   Is there any evidence to show that the lack of opportunity to participate in all areas of the curriculum is causing the child to be anxious?

5   Can you distinguish between the needs of the pupil in curriculum terms and the need for physical access to the classroom? That is, the needs which are related to the child's management of the physical disability and the ways in which the disability affects access to learning.

6   Can you demonstrate how the school has used information technology as well as aids to facilitate independence?

Children with Sensory Impairment: Hearing or Visual Difficulties

1   Can you explain how the school has used the advice of outside specialists?

2   Can you detail the advice given by educational, medical and social agencies?

3   Have you evidence to demonstrate that all staff who teach the child have been advised as to the nature and extent of loss and level of the child's functional vision or hearing and use of personal equipment?

4   Can you show how much you have explored the use and value of information technology?

Children with Speech and Language Difficulties

1   Has the child's expressive and receptive language been measured and compared with the development of children of his/her own age?

2   Have you evidence that the child's communication difficulties impede his or her development in National Curriculum subjects or other areas of the school curriculum?

3   Does the speech or language problem cause any difficulties with social relationships?

4   Is there any evidence of any associated sensory, intellectual or physical disabilities?

5   Does the child appear to be unduly stressed or anxious?

Children with Medical Problems

1   Can you provide evidence of how the child's medical problem impedes the child's learning opportunities?

2   Have you included records of the medical and parental advice you have

sought and how you have acted upon such advice?

3 Can you demonstrate how the staff have been advised of the medical problem, its implications for learning and its management?

4 Has the school established tried and tested procedures to ensure the child's safety?

5 Does the child appear to be unduly stressed or anxious?

Criteria for Assessing Levels of SEN

In the light of the criticism voiced in the HMI/Audit Commission Report (DES, 1992) about the lack of clarity regarding the level of SEN which should trigger the assessment process, some LEAs are developing criteria for the guidance of schools in determining which children should be referred for statutory assessments. In examples examined so far it would seem that there is a tendency to use standardised measures such as intelligence quotients and attainment quotients as well as employing simple checklists which suggest limits of attainment. For example, one criterion could be that a child cannot read a set number of sight words or perform certain mathematical calculations at a given chronological age. It has to be said that, far from being helpful to schools as was intended, many schools are viewing such criteria as LEA devices for turning down requests for statutory assessments since the criteria which are being suggested set low expectations for all pupils. This is a great pity since there is a widely accepted need for greater objectivity in deciding which pupils would benefit from statutory assessments and statements of SEN. Although the application of simplistic criteria is unlikely to improve this situation it is perhaps the first step along the road to greater objectivity.

STAGES OF STATUTORY ASSESSMENT

It is essential for all SEN co-ordinators to understand the process of statutory assessment so that they can manage their schools' responses to it. They should be aware of the steps to be taken and the order in which information is considered and responses made. Below is an outline of the process.

1 Parent or school makes a request for an assessment.

2 LEA responds by informing parents that an assessment is being considered.

There follows a 6-week period during which the LEA will be examining the evidence submitted in support of the request.

3 LEA gives notice to parent that they have decided not to undertake an assessment. The LEA must write to the school and parent giving reasons for their decision.

4 Parents may make an appeal to the SEN tribunal (see Rabinowicz and Friel, 1994).

or

5 LEA gives notice that they will proceed with the assessment. At this point reasons for the decision together with an explanation of the process should be communicated to the parent.

Once a decision to assess has been made, LEAs will collect written evidence from various agencies, namely:

- parents;
- school;
- educational psychologists;
- special needs support service;
- health authority;
- social services;
- any other evidence which the child, parent, LEA or any other agency considers desirable.

Schools should be able to provide additional information to complement the information already provided in their original request for assessment. Care must be taken that this evidence does not conflict with evidence previously given but is viewed as an update of developments since the original evidence was submitted.

All this advice should be received by the LEA within 6 weeks of the request. This leaves the LEA a further 4 weeks in which to make the decision whether to write a statement or not. According to the Code, the criteria generally used in determining whether a statement of special needs should be written is 'when the LEA conclude that all the special educational provision necessary to meet the child's needs cannot reasonably be provided within the resources normally available to mainstream schools in the area' (DfE, 1994, p. 79).

In coming to a decision about whether to draw up a statement, the LEA will examine the evidence presented in the statutory reports and compare it with the evidence presented by the school previously. For example, they will look for any information which may indicate that the school could meet the child's needs with advice or special equipment, thus obviating the need for a statement. They will ask:

- Is the special needs provision indicated by the statutory assessment outside the provision which can reasonably be expected to be made by the school? or,
- Are there approaches which the school could adopt and manage from within its own resources?

If the indicators are such that the LEA believes that more can be done without additional resources, then they must write to the parent a *note in lieu of a statement* in which they set out the reasons for their conclusions, with supporting evidence from the statutory assessment. All the advice which has been collected during that assessment must be forwarded to the parents, and, with the agreement of the parents, to the child's school. It is intended that this information can influence the strategies that the school will use in meeting the child's needs. It is therefore hoped that the decision not to issue a statement will not be regarded negatively by parents since what has been learnt from the assessment will be used to ensure that the child's special needs are provided for. When, and only when, the LEA is satisfied that the assessment and provision being made by the school is appropriate, *but* the child is not responding or progressing sufficiently well, will the LEA consider what further provision may be needed.

Even then the LEA will wish to satisfy itself that the further provision cannot be met from the school resources. If such provision is 'advisory' in nature rather than 'teaching support' – a small piece of equipment rather than expensive equipment, occasional support for personal care rather than daily support from a non-teaching assistant – then the LEA may expect the school to use the monies allocated through its LMS formula to make this provision.

Where the further provision is substantial then the LEA may conclude that the school could not reasonably be expected to make that provision from its own resources or funds. In such a case the LEA may decide: (1) to provide funding for the additional provision to be made within the mainstream school; or (2) that the child should attend a special facility. The details of these arrangements will be provided in a written statement of special educational needs.

WRITING A STATEMENT

A statement will be written according to a set format which can be found on page 85 of the Code of Practice. This is summarised below:

- *Part 1 (introduction)*. This will contain child's names, address, date of birth, home language and religion, and parents' address(es).
- *Part 2 (special educational needs)*. This section will contain a description of all the child's special needs as identified in the assessment documents.

- *Part 3 (special educational provision)*. This section will outline the SEN provision to be made, the educational objectives and arrangements for monitoring progress in preparation for an Annual Review of the Statement.
- *Part 4 (placement)*. The type and name of school or arrangements to be made otherwise than at school are specified.
- *Part 5 (non-educational needs)*. Other needs of the child as agreed between health and social services, other agencies and the LEA are specified.
- *Part 6 (non-educational provision)*. Non-educational provision to meet the needs specified in part 5 are stated.

The LEA must now draw up a proposed statement in which part 4, 'placement', is not completed. This must be forwarded to the parent together will all the evidence which was collected during the process of assessment. At the same time the LEA must inform the parents, in a way prescribed in part A of the Schedule to the Regulations, of the arrangements for naming an appropriate school. Copies of the proposed statement should also be sent to all those contributing to the advice previously given. An SEN co-ordinator should expect to receive a copy. The naming of a school must comply with three conditions. Namely:

- that the child's needs can be met there;
- that it is compatible with the interests of children already attending that school;
- that it is an efficient use of LEA resources.

This is an area where schools should be aware of the possible conflict between parents and an LEA. What may be seen as an efficient use of LEA resources may not be seen by the parent as the choice they wish to make. Although this section is well documented within the Code, SEN co-ordinators are advised to be sensitive about this issue.

It should also be noted that, although the LEA has a duty to consult with a school which they intend to name in a statement, the school's governing body cannot refuse to admit a child merely because he or she has special educational needs.

Once any amendments have been made to a proposed statement, a final statement should be issued as soon as possible and the 'provision' on the statement arranged. Some LEAs now provide a cash limit with the statement of SEN and schools must account for how this is used to meet the conditions of the statement. For example, the LEA may determine that from the evidence presented the child is deemed to have 'moderate learning difficulties'. Such a decision will attract a specified sum of money which is transferred to the school. This is considered to be additional to the monies from the LMS

CHILD

PART 1: INTRODUCTION

Surname _____ Other names _____ John _____

Home address _____ _____

_____ Sex _____

_____ Religion _____

Date of birth _____ 24.9.82 _____ Home language ____ English ____

CHILD'S PARENT OR PERSON RESPONSIBLE

Surname _____ Other names _____

Home address _____ _____

_____ Relationship to child _____

_____ _____

Telephone no. _____

PART 2: SPECIAL EDUCATIONAL NEEDS

John is of average ability, but his academic progress has been restricted by
behavioural difficulties. He lacks motivation, his concentration is limited and
he cannot complete tasks without close supervision. His poor relationships
with his peers is typified by verbal and physical aggression and he finds it
very difficult to conform to the social expectations of a mainstream school.
Although John displays difficult and challenging behaviour in school, at home
and in the community he can be pleasant and responsive when being taught
individually.

PART 3: SPECIAL EDUCATIONAL PROVISION

1   Participation in the National Curriculum, suitably differentiated to take
     account of his academic difficulties.
2   Firm consistent management within clearly defined and applied
     behavioural guidelines.
3   Implementation of a behaviour modification programme which is based
     on a reward system and is short term in its objectives.
4   Advice and support from an Educational Psychologist on behaviour
     modification programmes.
5   Structured programmes in basic skills, particularly in reading, spelling,
     writing and number work.
6   A full review of progress and provision in two terms.

Figure 5.1 Parts 1, 2 and 3 of a specimen statement

formula, and the school must be accountable for its use. In one LEA the formula indicates that a school should spend 5 per cent of the age-weighted pupil unit and 50 per cent of its compensatory allowance on pupils with special educational needs. Advisers/inspectors within that LEA will expect schools to be able to account for the portion of the formula available to an individual pupil together with the additional sum noted above and will examine ways in which that money has been used to meet the requirements of the statement.

The SEN co-ordinator will be responsible for ensuring that the school arranges the provision as written on the statement and must ensure that those arrangements are monitored on a regular basis. For example, in Figure 5.1, which represents parts 1, 2 and 3 of a specimen statement, the information in part 2 indicates that John is considered to be of below average ability and that he has behavioural difficulties. His concentration is limited, he lacks motivation and requires close supervision to complete tasks. Evidence for this can be seen in poor relationships with his peers, verbal and physical aggression and difficulty in conforming to social requirements.These problems will have been highlighted in the evidence collected during the statutory assessment. This evidence will be available to the school since copies of all the reports submitted during the assessment will be forwarded to them, with parental approval.

In part 3, the statement indicates the provision which the LEA believes should be made in order to improve John's learning and behavioural difficulties. Whether the school agrees with these findings or not, they *must* be implemented. During the review, at the end of two terms the LEA will expect to see full documented evidence of:

- the action taken by the school;
- John's responses to those actions;
- the learning programmes established;
- John's progress or otherwise;
- involvement of educational psychology services;
- involvement of support staff.

Points to Ensure

The co-ordinator must ensure that:

1 *John is participating in the National Curriculum, and that his lessons are differentiated to meet his needs.* This will mean that all teachers must have a detailed understanding of his needs and of the most appropriate teaching methods and resources to use. This could involve the SEN

co-ordinator in arranging some form of INSET for staff.

2   *All staff employ consistent management strategies and that behavioural guidelines are provided to assist them.* The co-ordinator will need to arrange for the guidelines to be written and discussed with all staff, in order to gain staff agreement to a course of action and a set of responses. For pupils with problems like John's, it is important that all staff respond to his behaviour in a consistent way. This reduces the opportunities for John to play one person off against another.

3   *A behaviour modification programme is developed and used with John which operates on rewards rather than punishments and has short-term expectations.* The co-ordinator will need to determine what kind of rewards John is likely to respond to, and the length of time he can sustain his attempts to gain that reward. This may be as short as one lesson, or a morning or a day. Not all teachers are in favour of such strategies, and use the argument that pupils should not be rewarded for behaving in the way we would expect all pupils to behave. The significance here is that the LEA, through the statement, has decided that this is a course of action it wants to see implemented.

4   *Advice and support is sought from an educational psychologist.* Even if the SEN co-ordinator is very familiar with the development of behaviour modification programmes he or she must seek advice and support from an educational psychologist, or, alternatively, the educational psychologist can assist the co-ordinator with designing such a programme.

5   *John is provided with structured programmes in reading, spelling, writing and number work.* The co-ordinator will need to undertake additional assessments to determine the current levels of John's particular needs in the areas of the curriculum identified as weaknesses. Arrangements must then be put in place for John to be taught using structured programmes and for staff to be aware that these programmes are in use. This may necessitate the use of in-school support strategies or withdrawal from classes for individual attention.

6   *All aspects of the special arrangements for John are well documented and regularly reviewed.* This will mean keeping ongoing records up to date which indicate the success or otherwise of what is happening; any changes that have been made or need to be made and the current situation. Records of any involvement with parents and educational support agencies should be contained within the evidence.

In LEAs where a cash entitlement is transferred to the school, evidence will need to be kept to show how that money has been spent. In John's case it might well be spent to buy in the services of an educational psychologist (although in some LEAs this is still an LEA-funded provision) or to buy in a teacher to deliver the individual help which the teaching programmes might demand. In one LEA some schools are using internal monitoring forms such as that shown in A15 in the Appendices where part (a) is summarised from part 2 of the statement, part (b) is copied from part 3 of the statement and part (c) is the school's administrative or organisational record of how it is meeting its statutory obligations and using the earmarked funding. Other schools are considering using IEP programmes, similar to those presented in Chapters Three and Four, to establish programmes and monitor progress of pupils with statements.

ANNUAL REVIEWS

LEAs have the powers to review statements at any time during a year, but they must review a statement annually as a minimum requirement.

Purpose

The annual review should aim to evaluate the child's progress and to review the special provision which was outlined in the statement. It should further consider whether, in the light of the review, any changes need to be made to the statement or whether the statement can cease to be maintained.

Procedure

All annual reviews up to the child's 14th birthday are likely to be conducted by the school, though initiated by the LEA. Reviews after the child's 14th birthday will be managed by the LEA who will involve other agencies who are concerned with the child's needs after school age. The procedure for annual reviews is as follows:

1   LEA writes to school, copy to parents, to request that:
    (a) head teacher convenes a review meeting;
    (b) head teacher writes a review report.

Note: The head teacher must be given at least 2 months' notice of the date by which the report must be returned to the LEA and the head teacher can delegate his or her functions to any teacher in the school. In many schools this will be the SEN co-ordinator.

2   The head teacher invites the following people to the review meeting:
    (a) a representative of the LEA;
    (b) child's parents or carer;
    (c) the SEN co-ordinator or other teacher responsible for the child's SEN provision;

(d) any agency which the LEA tells the head teacher to invite, such as a representative of the health authority;

(e) any agency which the head teacher wishes to be present.

3　In preparation for the meeting the head teacher must:

(a) request written advice from all those to be invited to the review, including parents;

(b) circulate a copy of all the advice received to all those invited to the meeting at least 2 weeks before the date of that meeting and invite comments from those unable to attend.

The Review Meeting

The meeting will normally take place in the child's school and will be chaired by the head teacher, SEN co-ordinator, or other teacher to whom responsibility has been delegated. The meeting will address the following issues.

1　parents' views of the past year's progress and their hopes for the future;

2　pupils' views of their progress and future aims;

3　the school's view, together with evidence of what progress has been made towards meeting the objectives and targets as agreed in the original statement or last review, as the case may be;

4　any significant changes in the child's circumstances which may affect future progress;

5　appropriateness of current provision in meeting child's needs;

6　future educational targets against which the child's progress will be assessed at the next review;

7　any further action required, if so by whom;

8　whether the statement is still appropriate, or requires modification or whether the LEA ceases to maintain it.

Amendments to the statement

A review meeting may recommend amendments to a statement if:

1　important new needs have come to light which are not recorded on the statement;

2　needs which are recorded on the statement are no longer relevant;

3　provision should be altered to meet a child's changing needs;

4　a child's needs would be more appropriately met in another school.

The Review Report

Following the annual review meeting the head teacher must write a report which summarises the outcomes of the meeting. The discussion during the meeting, together with the written evidence for the meeting, will form the basis of the report. Some LEAs offer guidance on the format of the review report, so, where available, schools can make use of this.

The report should be circulated to all those concerned in the reviews by the date specified by the LEA's initial letter to the head teacher. The LEA will then examine the review report and review the child's statement in the light of that report, make their own recommendations and convey them to all those invited to the review meeting.

Annual review from ages 14–19

In general the details described above for the review meeting and report are applicable to the first review following the 14th birthday of a young person with SEN with the following amendments:

1   The LEA will convene the review meeting.
2   The LEA must ensure that other agencies, such as social services, are aware of the importance of the meeting.
3   The LEA must invite the careers service to be represented.
4   The LEA will prepare the review report and include in it a *transition plan*. This is then circulated to all who have been invited to the meeting together with any others the LEA considers appropriate. For example, it might be relevant to forward a copy to the Further Education Funding Council (FEFC) where a decision might need to be taken about specialist college provision.

The transition plan
The purpose of the transition plan is to bring together education services with all those agencies who will affect the child's transition to adult life. It is likely that many children with special educational needs will require the services of agencies within the community, such as social services and the careers service, to facilitate a quality of life and their access to continuing education and vocational training.

The transition plan must address a number of issues, a comprehensive list of which can be found on page 118 of the Code, but which includes:

1   *School.*
    (a) What are the young person's curriculum needs at this time?

   (b) How can the curriculum assist the young person with the transition
       to adult life?
2 *Professionals.*
   (a) How can colleagues from various agencies plan a coherent package
       of support?
   (b) Which professionals need to be involved?
   (c) Are there any health or welfare needs?
   (d) What technological aids might be needed?
   (e) How can information be transferred efficiently between all involved?
   (f) Is education after age 16 appropriate?
3 *Family.*
   (a) What do parents expect of their son or daughter's adult life?
   (b) What can they contribute in helping their child develop personal and
       social skills?
   (c) What support will parents need in the future?
4 *The young person.*
   (a) What information do they need to make informed choices?
   (b) How can they contribute to their own transition plan?

It is expected that every effort will be made to ensure that the transition from
school to adult life will be as smooth as possible and in the young person's
best interests.

Summary

1 Transfer from stage 3 to stage 4 requires detailed evidence of previous actions.
2 The management of stages 4 and 5 will rest with the LEA.
3 A statutory assessment will require up-to-date reports from a number of
   sources including parents.
4 The decision whether to write a statement or not depends upon whether
   the evidence indicates that, although the school has acted properly and is
   making appropriate provision, the child is not making progress.
5 A statement will indicate the additional resources needed as well as the
   expected provision.
6 The SEN co-ordinator is likely to be the person who must ensure that the
   expectations of a statement are being met and are monitored on a regular
   basis.
7 All statements must be reviewed at least annually according to the
   procedures laid down in the Code.
8 The first annual review after the child's 14th birthday achieves a new
   significance and must include a transition plan.
9 The Code expects all relevant agencies to work together in harmony.

CHAPTER SIX

Effective Strategies for Involving Parents

INTRODUCTION

The Code of Practice emphasises the importance of establishing a partnership with parents. It suggests that this partnership 'has a crucial bearing on the child's educational progress and the effectiveness of any school-based action' (DfE, 1994, p. 12). It goes on to say (p. 13) that:

> Children's progress will be diminished if their parents are not seen as partners in the educational process with unique knowledge to impart. Professional help can seldom be effective unless it builds on parents' capacity to be involved and unless parents consider that professionals take account of what they say and treat their views and anxieties as intrinsically important.

An essential aspect of the partnership envisaged in the Code is that it must be based on mutual respect. For example, it requires parents and teachers to listen to each other and give due consideration to each other's views. In this way an effective collaborative working relationship can be established. In this relationship, teachers should be aware of addressing parents' needs and of acknowledging the various ways they can contribute to the development and education of their children with special needs. Teachers should encourage parents to recognise their responsibilities towards their children and to understand that optimum progress will be made when they work in partnership with teachers and other professionals. In order for such a partnership to become a reality, schools need to produce and implement written policies on parent involvement which take into account parents' rights and responsibilities regarding the education of their children.

This chapter documents the increasing importance of parental involvement in education which has resulted from the additional rights given to parents in legislation enacted since 1979. A model for parent involvement is presented in order to provide guidance to schools in developing their policy and practice for working in partnership with parents. The model highlights different aspects of parent involvement which need to be considered in developing such a policy. Facilitating the participation of parents in the assessment and review of their children's progress is highlighted. Steps for the development of a written school policy for working with parents are discussed and the issues which need to be addressed in such a policy are outlined. Finally, the competencies needed by teachers in order to work in partnership with parents and to collaborate effectively with other professionals are considered. These include the relevant attitudes and knowledge as well as listening skills, assertion skills and the skills involved in using a 3-stage problem-solving model of counselling.

INCREASED PARENTAL RIGHTS REGARDING CHILDREN WITH SEN

The benefits of involving parents in their children's education first gained widespread acknowledgement from teachers in the 1960s following publication of the Plowden Report (1967) and reports on the projects conducted in educational priority areas, most of which involved working closely with parents. Legislation enacted since 1979 has had the effect of increasing the importance of parental involvement in education since parents' rights have been substantially extended (Statham et al., 1989; Wolfendale, 1992). The additional rights given to parents in this period are summarised below.

1980 Education Act
In this legislation parents were granted the right to choose the school they want to send their children to. Parents were also given the right to be represented on the governing bodies of schools. In addition, school governors and Local Education Authorities (LEAs) were required to provide written information to parents on such things as: admission criteria; the curriculum; examination results; discipline; and school organisation.

1981 Education Act
This was the Act in which many of the recommendations of the Warnock Report (DES, 1978) were embodied. It was aimed solely at children with special needs. The Act gave parents the right to request the LEA to conduct

a formal assessment of their children's special educational needs. It requires parent involvement in the assessment process and in annual reviews of their children's progress. It also gives parents the right to appeal against LEA decisions. Further, it made it clear that parents' wishes should be taken into account when deciding whether or not to integrate children with special needs into ordinary schools.

1986 Education Act

The first of two Education Acts passed in 1986 required increased parental representation on the governing bodies of schools. Governors were required to present an annual report to parents and to have a meeting with parents at the school in order to discuss the report.

1988 Education Act

This Act granted parents the right to send their children to any school of their choice so long as it has room for them. It also required that parents are sent an annual report on their children's progress. In addition, it gave schools the opportunity of opting out of LEA control if a majority of parents voted in favour of this.

1992 Education Act

This Act set out new procedures for the inspection of schools, in which parents have an increased role. Parents have the right to meet with inspectors before the inspection to discuss any issues they wish. School staff and governors are not allowed to be present unless their children attend the school. Also, all parents are sent a questionnaire by the inspectors asking for their comments on the school. In addition, inspectors are expected to have discussions with parents on a wide range of issues concerning schools, including the way parents are involved in the identification and assessment of special educational needs and annual reviews of statements (Stone, 1993). Finally, parents have the right to receive a summary report on the results of the school inspection.

1993 Education Act

The Code of Practice (which provides guidance on the implementation of the 1993 Act) emphasises the importance for schools of establishing partnerships with parents. It requires that schools should have written *policy and procedures* for:

- acting on parental concerns;
- involving parents when teachers express concerns about their child;
- incorporating parents' views in assessment and reviews of progress.

It also requires that schools provide parents with *information* on:

- the schools' policy for special educational needs (SEN);
- the support available for children with SEN within the school and LEA;
- the services provided by local authorities for children with SEN;
- parents' rights to be involved in assessment and decision making;
- voluntary organisations which can provide guidance or support.

In addition, it requires that schools ensure that parents have *access* to this information by providing:

- information in the community languages spoken by parents for whom English is not their first language;
- information on tape for parents who have literacy difficulties;
- a parents' room or other arrangements to help parents feel comfortable about coming to the school.

The effect of the 1993 Education Act will therefore be to further strengthen parental influence over the education of their children.

The increasing emphasis on parents' rights which has evolved through the above Education Acts means that schools can no longer afford *not* to work closely with parents. It is therefore essential that schools have a carefully considered policy on involving parents, including those who have children with SEN, in a variety of ways. In order to consider the wide variety of forms of parent involvement which need to be taken into account by a school policy, a model intended to guide the practice of working with parents is presented next.

MODEL TO GUIDE THE PRACTICE OF PARENT INVOLVEMENT

A model for conceptualising parent involvement has been developed by considering ideas from several writers on the topic (Bastiani, 1989; Kroth, 1985; Lombana, 1983; Wolfendale, 1992) and by gaining feedback from numerous groups of parents and teachers. The model was originally devised with teachers and parents of children with special needs in mind (Hornby, 1989) but it was subsequently realised that, with slight adaptations, it was equally applicable to all teachers and parents (Hornby, 1990). The model for

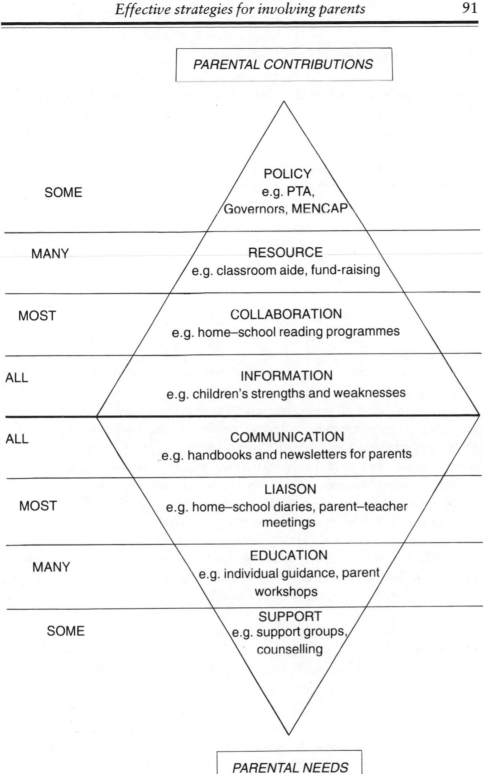

Figure 6.1 Model for parent involvement

parent involvement is presented in Figure 6.1.

The model consists of two pyramids, one representing a hierarchy of parents' needs, the other a hierarchy of parents' strengths or possible contributions. Both pyramids demonstrate visually the different levels of needs and contributions of parents. Thus, while all parents have some needs and some potential contributions which can be utilised, a smaller number have intense need for guidance, or the capability of making an extensive contribution. The model also suggests that, for parents' needs at a higher level, more time and expertise is required by teachers in order to meet these needs. Similarly, the parents who make a greater contribution require a higher level of expertise and time available. Each of the components of the model will now be outlined.

Contributions by Parents

Information

All parents can contribute valuable information about their children because they have known them throughout their lives and have been the ones who have participated in all previous contacts with professionals in order to assess and plan for meeting their children's needs. Information concerning children's likes and dislikes, strengths and weaknesses, along with any relevant medical details can be gathered by teachers at parent–teacher meetings or by telephone. Many parents feel more comfortable on their own territory and generally appreciate it when teachers offer to visit them. This also provides an opportunity to observe how parents cope with their children at home and to learn about any relevant family circumstances. Making full use of parents' knowledge of their children not only leads to more effective professional practice, it also makes parents feel that they have been listened to and that an active interest has been taken in their children.

Collaboration

Most parents are willing and able to contribute more than just information. Most parents are able to collaborate with teachers by reinforcing classroom programmes at home, such as in home–school reading programmes (Topping, 1986). However, some parents, at some times, are not willing to carry out work at home with their children. This can be very frustrating for teachers since they realise that collaboration between home and school generally results in children making greater progress, so that children whose parents do not work closely with them are likely to develop more slowly. However, it is considered that teachers have to accept that some parents at some points in time are simply not able to collaborate in this way. Probably this is because their resources are already fully committed in coping with their children at home, so they are not able to do anything extra. At a later time family circumstances may change and parents may then want to become more involved in their children's education. Professionals must respect parents' rights to make this decision in consideration of the wider needs of their families. So, while involvement in home–school programmes, or other requests for parents to carry out work with their children at home, should always be offered to all parents, including those who have not collaborated in the past, it should be accepted that a small proportion of parents will not participate.

Resource

Many parents have the time and ability to act as voluntary teacher aides, either assisting in the classroom, or in the preparation of materials, or in fund raising. Others may have special skills which they can contribute such as helping prepare newsletters, in craft activities, or in curriculum areas in which they have a special talent. Some parents may have the time, skills and knowledge to provide support to other parents either informally or perhaps through participation in self-help or support groups such as parent-to-parent schemes (see Hornby, 1994).

In these times of contracting professional resources teachers should make sure that they make optimum use of this valuable voluntary resource. However, too often this doesn't happen, as is illustrated by an incident which occurred when the parent involvement model was presented to a group of parents and teachers at a special school. When the possibility of parents acting as a resource was mentioned, the head teacher commented that parents were encouraged to come into the school to help in this way. Immediately, a parent responded that her child had been in the school for 3 years and she didn't know about this. This incident highlights the fact that invitations for parents to help at the school need to be repeated at least annually by such means as newsletters.

It is often the case that parents also benefit from acting as a resource. They may acquire knowledge which is helpful to their understanding of their own children. In addition, they are often observed to gain in confidence through helping others rather than always being the ones to receive help.

Policy

Some parents are able to contribute their expertise through membership of parent or professional organisations. This includes being a school governor, a lay inspector, a member of the PTA, or being involved in a parent support or advocacy group. Others have the time and ability to provide in-service training for professionals by speaking at conferences or workshops, or by writing about their experiences (e.g. Featherstone, 1981). Parents can influence school policy on children with special needs through their involvement as a governor or PTA member. They can also sometimes influence government policy on children with special educational needs through their involvement in groups such as MENCAP and the Spastics Society. Teachers should continually be on the look-out for parents who can contribute in these ways so that their abilities can be used to the full.

Needs of Parents

Communication

All parents need to have effective channels of communication with the teachers who work with their children. They need information about the organisation and requirements of the school as it affects their children. They need to know when their children are to be assessed, their progress reviewed and when a change of placement is being considered. That is, all parents need to know about their rights and responsibilities. This can be provided through handbooks or regular newsletters written especially for parents.

Parents need to feel that they can contact the school at any time when they have a concern about their child. Some parents prefer to communicate by telephone, others would rather call in to see the teacher face to face, while still others find that contact through written notes or home–school diaries suits them best. Therefore, teachers need to ensure that a wide range of communication channels are open to parents. However, the most important factor in maintaining good communication is the openness to parents which schools demonstrate through their contacts with parents. The attitude of choice has often been referred to as an 'open door policy' in which parents feel comfortable about contacting or going into the school when they have a concern (Harding and Pike, 1988).

Liaison

Most parents want to know how their children are getting on at school. They want to find out what their children have achieved and whether they are having any difficulties. They regard teachers as the main source of information on their children's performance at school and therefore need to have a working partnership with them. Teachers can facilitate this by keeping in regular contact with parents through such means as telephone calls, home visits, home–school notebooks, weekly report forms and by meeting with parents at school (for a detailed discussion of these forms of liaison see Hornby, in press).

Teachers are often disappointed that some parents do not come to parent–teacher meetings at school, thereby giving the impression that they are not interested in how their children are getting on. However, there are usually other reasons for them not turning up, such as the difficulties involved in getting a baby-sitter, the overwhelming demands of looking after their family, or anxieties about coming to the school which are related to their own negative school experiences. It is important, then, for teachers to find other ways of liaising with these parents, perhaps by having regular telephone contacts or home visits.

Education

Many parents appreciate receiving guidance from teachers on promoting their children's progress or dealing with specific difficulties. Many parents of children with SEN are interested in participating in parent education programmes or parent workshops which are widely reported in the literature (e.g. Hornby and Murray, 1983). However, some parents will not want to take part in such programmes, for a variety of reasons. There will be those who, at a certain point in time, feel confident about the way they are parenting their children with SEN and don't see the need for parent education. Later, when their children reach a different developmental stage they may think differently. For other parents, there will be practical difficulties such as transport. However, a substantial number of parents are interested in being involved in parent workshops and most of those who do participate get a tremendous amount out of it. Ideally, then, opportunities for receiving individual guidance or taking part in group parent education should be made available to all parents.

It seems that the most effective format for parent education is one which combines guidance about promoting children's development with opportunities for parents to discuss their concerns (Pugh and De'Ath, 1984). Parent education programmes which involve a group of parents, and employ a workshop format, easily lend themselves to providing a combination of educational input and sharing of concerns. This type of format enables parents to learn new skills and gain confidence through talking to other parents and teachers.

Support

Some parents, at some times, are in need of supportive counselling, even though they may not actually request it. This support can be provided either individually or in groups such as self-help groups or the parent workshops mentioned above. Although such support should be available to all parents, the majority of parents seldom need extensive counselling. In the past it has often been assumed that the greatest need of parents of children with SEN is counselling in order to help them come to terms with their child's disability. This has led to an over-emphasis on this aspect of parent involvement to the detriment of the other aspects, such as communication and liaison, which have been discussed above. The fact is, that if parents have good channels of communication and regular liaison with teachers, coupled with the opportunity to receive guidance about their children whenever they need it, then only a few of them will need extensive counselling at any particular time.

Whereas most British parents are reluctant to seek the help of professional counsellors, they will approach their children's teachers in search of guidance or counselling for the problems which concern them. Teachers should therefore have a level of basic counselling skills sufficient to be good listeners and to help parents solve everyday problems (see Hornby, 1994). They should also be able to refer parents on to professional counsellors or support groups when problems raised are beyond their level of competence.

FACILITATING PARENTAL INVOLVEMENT IN ASSESSMENTS AND REVIEWS

All the above aspects of work with parents are important in designing a comprehensive scheme of parental involvement for each school. However, certain aspects of parental involvement are crucial in that they are mandated by the Code of Practice. These are the areas of parental involvement in assessments of children with SEN and reviews of their progress, including statutory assessments and annual reviews of statements. The importance placed on this in the Code is emphasised by the following quotation,

> School-based arrangements should ensure that assessment reflects a sound and comprehensive knowledge of a child and his or her responses to a variety of carefully planned and recorded actions *which take account of the wishes, feelings and knowledge of parents at all stages*.
>
> (DfE, 1994, pp. 12–13)

Wolfendale (1992) suggests that assessment should be conducted by means of a partnership between parents and teachers. In the early stages it should encompass the sharing of information with both parents and teachers setting out their opinions and concerns about children. Later, more specific data on the child's development are collected by parents and teachers by such means as observations, checklists and tests. The information collected is then shared in a parent–teacher meeting so that an assessment of the child's behaviour and attainments in both home and school settings is achieved. Viewing parental and teacher assessment data as complementary in this way leads to a more open sharing of concerns and ideas between the two and thereby promotes the development of a collaborative partnership.

What Parents Want from Assessments

Parents of children with SEN typically suffer considerable anxiety about assessments conducted with their children. They realise the importance of the results of such assessments in making decisions about appropriate placements, about the amount of specialist help the child will receive and about the likely future development of the child. Most parents are therefore very keen to know about any assessments their children are to undergo and like to receive feedback on such assessments as soon a possible afterwards.

Wolfendale (1992) suggests that parents typically have five main expectations when their children are assessed:

1   They want to know what steps will be taken as a result of the assessment and what they can do to help.
2   They want to be able to discuss their children's past performance with their current teacher.
3   They want to hear constructive comments on their children's current rate of progress in relation to their previous achievements and to the performance of other children.
4   They want to know what strategies teachers are going to use in order to remediate their children's weaknesses.
5   They seek confirmation that their children are happy and making progress in their current school.

Broadfoot (1989) reports some research which suggests that the information parents want from teachers needs to be:

* *Objective*. That is, comments which can be substantiated rather than based on speculation.
* *Constructive*. That is, information which suggests strategies for improving progress.
* *Significant*. That is, information which focuses on important areas of development.
* *Succinct*. That is, comments which are brief and to the point.
* *Goal-related*. That is, information which can be related to parents' goals for their children.
* *Broadly based*. That is, information which focuses on a broad view of their children's needs.

What Parents Can Contribute to Assessments

Wolfendale (1992) considers that the quality of parental contributions to assessments is equivalent to that of professionals. She believes that parents can make an invaluable input to the assessment process for several reasons:

- Parents are able to make realistic appraisals of their children.
- Parents have extensive knowledge of their children's development from birth onwards.
- Parents have intimate knowledge of the family circumstances which affect the child.
- Parents have knowledge of other factors related to the wider social environment in which the family lives which have an impact on the child.
- Parents can supply knowledge of children's behaviour in the home setting which may well be different to that at school.
- Information from parents complements that from professionals and therefore can serve to highlight concerns regarding progress.

Increasing the Effectiveness of Parental Involvement in Assessments and Reviews

Since involving parents in the assessment and review processes is likely to significantly improve the quality of information available it is important to attempt to optimise the effectiveness of parental involvement in these processes. That is, rather than parents being seen as recipients of information who are asked to comment on assessment data produced by professionals they should be seen as active partners in the process of collecting and reviewing assessment data. Meetings with parents to discuss assessments and reviews should therefore be efficiently organised and conducted. At these meetings parents should be viewed as valuable partners in the educational process and every attempt made to ensure that rather than feeling intimidated they feel empowered to participate to the fullest extent.

Guidelines for optimising the effectiveness of such meetings, which have been adapted from the work of several authors (Kroth, 1985; Simpson, 1990; Swap, 1993; Turnbull and Turnbull, 1986), are presented below. The guidelines are divided into three sections focusing on organising meetings, conducting meetings and reviewing meetings. Finally, specific ways of improving parental input into assessment and review meetings are described.

Organising meetings
1   It is preferable if the teacher's first contact with parents is not in a formal

meeting but is made by means of a home visit or an informal contact such as on an open day, so that some rapport has been established beforehand.

2 Notifying parents about meetings is usually best done by letters of invitation sent home at least 2 weeks in advance, if possible followed up by less formal reminders, such as a brief note in a child's school bag or a short telephone call, 2 or 3 days before the meeting. Invitations need to clearly specify the purpose, place, time and length of time allotted for the meeting.

3 Along with the invitation parents should be sent some guidelines to help them prepare for the meeting. Kroth (1985) suggests that most parents appreciate this because it conveys a message that parental input is welcome. Guidelines for parents could include:
   (a) making a list of questions to ask, e.g. about the child's progress and behaviour;
   (b) being prepared to ask for clarification of any unfamiliar terminology which is used;
   (c) being prepared to comment on children's activities at home, e.g. hobbies and interests;
   (d) being prepared to comment on what limits are set at home, e.g. regarding bedtime;
   (e) being prepared to comment on factors which may affect the child at school, e.g. child's health;
   (f) talking to children to check whether they have any concerns about school.

4 It is important to arrange to use the most suitable venue available. Ideally, comfortable chairs should be used, arranged so that there are no physical barriers such as a desk between participants at the meeting. Also, distractions should be avoided and privacy maintained by keeping the door closed and having a 'Do Not Disturb' sign on the outside of it.

5 Before the meeting it is useful to review children's records, assessment data and work done at school. Typical examples of children's work can be selected in order to show parents at the meeting.

6 In general it is best to invite all other professionals who have input into the child's educational programme and to appraise them about what information they need to bring to the meeting. It is also important to liaise with colleagues who cannot attend the meeting in order to get their views on the child's progress.

7 Where appropriate, pupils can be involved in the meeting along with their parents. If this is not considered appropriate then children should be told about the purpose of the meeting and given the opportunity of having input into the agenda.

8 A tentative agenda for the meeting should be drawn up.

Conducting meetings

1 In order to establish rapport, when parents arrive time should be spent welcoming them and making them feel at ease. They should be thanked for coming and encouraged to ask questions or comment at any time during the meeting.

2 Participants should be reminded of the time limits set for the meeting since there is good evidence that setting time limits helps to reduce irrelevant discussions (Simpson, 1990).

3 The purpose of the meeting can be stated and the agenda items proposed by the teacher can be listed. Parents should be asked if there are other issues or concerns they would like to discuss at the meeting. Parents' items can then be added to the agenda which should be dealt with in agreed priority order.

4 It is easier to build rapport in a meeting if notes are not taken during it. However, teachers often find it useful to note important details and list things they need to do after the meeting. Parents may also want to make notes. So the issue of note-taking should be discussed at the beginning of the meeting.

5 It is usually best to start on a positive note by stating the areas in which the child is doing well. Concerns the teacher has about difficulties the child is experiencing or creating should be stated clearly and specifically but with sensitivity.

6 In order to get parents to open up and share concerns and ideas teachers need to use the listening skills which are described in the following chapter.

7 Where parents and professionals disagree then the problem-solving procedure, which is discussed in the following chapter, should be used.

8 At the end of the meeting, the teacher should summarise the main points which have emerged and review the action which both parents and professionals have agreed to take.

9 Parents should be thanked for their participation and reminded that they can contact the teacher if they want to discuss any aspects of the meeting further.

Reviewing meetings

Following the meeting teachers have several tasks to complete in order to make best use of the outcome of the meeting.

1 A brief report should be written to summarise the main issues which were discussed and the decisions which emerged from the meeting. It should record the individuals responsible for carrying out each recommendation which was agreed upon.

2 The impact of any recommendations on children should be explained to

them and they should be given the opportunity to ask questions about the meeting.

3   Other colleagues should be informed about the outcome of the meeting and any recommendation relevant to their work with the child discussed with them.

4   Teachers need to plan for the implementation of the recommendations agreed at the meeting and for next review of progress.

5   Teachers should periodically solicit feedback from parents and other professionals regarding the effectiveness of meetings, perhaps by asking participants to complete a brief questionnaire which focuses on such things as: the suitability of the room used; the adequacy of the time available; the usefulness of information obtained; and the helpfulness of the recommendations made.

Assessments

Several examples of attempts to improve the effectiveness of parental input into the assessment of children have been reported by Wolfendale (1988 and 1992). These have involved the completion of diaries, observation charts, developmental checklists and parental profiles, by parents in collaboration with teachers, in order to assess the behaviour and development of children. Parental profiles have been used in situations as diverse as assessing children's progress prior to their entry into school as rising 5-year-olds and preparing material to present as the parental advice required for statutory assessments. In fact, the Code recognises the benefits of providing a structure for optimising written parental contributions to statutory assessments by providing guidelines on pages 72 and 73. Clearly, there is recognition of the benefits of providing parents with proformas to guide their input into the assessment process. It therefore seems expedient to use such proformas for all assessments conducted with children who have SEN. In order to address this suggestion, a sample proforma for use by parents for providing data on their children as part of an assessment is presented in the Appendices as A16. It is recognised that this proforma is a general one and may need to be adapted for children of different ages or to suit the particular situation for which it is to be used.

Progress reviews

An example of an attempt to improve the effectiveness of parental input into reviews of children's progress was reported by Hughes and Carpenter (1991). They describe the use of a Parents' Comments Form (PCF) devised to help parents organise their thoughts on their child's progress and needs in order to prepare them to contribute more meaningfully to the annual reviews of the child's statement of SEN. In an evaluation of the use of the PCF, with parents of children attending a special school for children with severe learning difficulties, it was reported that parents found the forms helpful in preparing for the review meetings and it was considered that this led to a more effective partnership between parents and teachers. A sample proforma (adapted from that suggested by Hughes and Carpenter) for use by parents for providing data on their children as part of a review of their progress is presented in the Appendices as A17. Inclusion of the above ideas on involving parents in assessments and reviews should be enshrined in each school's policy on parental involvement. The development of such a policy is discussed below.

DEVELOPING A SCHOOL POLICY FOR INVOLVING PARENTS

Policy regarding parental involvement is necessarily a part of each school's policy on SEN, which needs to be a written document presented to all parents, as discussed in earlier chapters. However, the importance of parental involvement may influence some schools to produce a separate written policy on working with parents. Either way the determination of a policy for parental involvement will need to be carefully considered by each school. Ideally, devising this policy should be something in which the whole school community is involved. A possible sequence for producing the policy could be as follows:

- all teachers at the school are involved in discussing the proposed content of the policy at a staff meeting or an in-service training day;
- a small group of staff are assigned to produce a draft of the policy;
- the draft policy is circulated to all staff, governors and PTA members for their comments;
- the draft policy is revised, based on feedback from these groups;
- the revised draft policy is discussed at full meetings of staff, governors and PTA and if no further revisions are needed it is adopted as school policy;
- the school policy on parental involvement is then presented to all parents either along with, or as part of, the policy on SEN.

Some aspects of what should be included in a school's policy on parental involvement are mandated by the Code, other aspects schools may wish to include in order to make public their policy on these issues. A checklist of elements which should be considered for inclusion in the school's policy is presented in Figure 6.2 and in the Appendices as A18.

COMPETENCIES NEEDED FOR EFFECTIVE PARENT INVOLVEMENT IN EDUCATION

In order to work effectively in partnership with parents, in fulfilling the various aspects included in the school's policy on parental involvement, teachers need to develop certain competencies. These are outlined below.

Attitudes

The attitudes which teachers require in order to work effectively with parents are ones which are consistent with the development of a collaborative partnership. To bring this about teachers should possess the basic underlying attitudes of genuineness, respect and empathy suggested by Carl Rogers (1980). They must be *genuine* in their relationships with parents. That is, they must come across as real people with their own strengths and weaknesses. For example, they should always be prepared to say that they 'don't know' when this is the case. Teachers should also show *respect* for parents. Parents' opinions and requests should always be given the utmost consideration. Most importantly, teachers should develop *empathy* with parents. They should try to see the child and family's situation from the point of view of the parents.

Another important attitude which professionals need is to have hopeful but realistic views about the likely progress and eventual prognosis of the children with SEN they work with. Parents need teachers to be optimistic but objective about their children's development. They need teachers to be people of integrity who will not shy away from being open and honest with them but will do this with sensitivity. Teachers should also have a problem-solving orientation. That is, they need to see every situation as one which can be improved, even if all the problems cannot be completely solved.

Knowledge

Teachers should have a good understanding of the process which parents typically experience in coming to terms with their child's SEN. They should also have a thorough knowledge of the dynamics of such families and of the various factors both inside and outside families which influence their functioning. They should have an understanding of the likely effects of a child with special educational needs on various members of the family, including siblings and grandparents. These aspects are discussed at length elsewhere (see Hornby, 1994).

Teachers should be aware of the various sources of additional finance which are available to parents of children with SEN including government benefits and grants from voluntary organisations. They need to be knowledgeable about the range of services which are available to parents and the agencies which supply them. They also need to be familiar with all other possible sources of help such as the parent support groups operating in the community where the family lives.

Finally, teachers should be knowledgeable about the different reactions to disability typical of different ethnic and cultural groups. They need to be sufficiently aware of the beliefs and customs of the ethnic groups with which they work to be able to adapt their approaches to parents so that they are culturally appropriate.

Skills

In order to work effectively with parents, teachers need good interpersonal communication skills (Turnbull and Turnbull, 1986). The most important of these skills are effective listening skills. These include the skills of attentiveness, passive listening, paraphrasing and active listening which are discussed in the following chapter.

Also important are basic counselling skills. Teachers require the ability to listen to what parents have to say, to help them gain a clearer understanding of the situation they face and to help them decide what action they should take. A 3-stage model of counselling, and the skills which teachers need in order to use it, are outlined in the next chapter.

Other interpersonal skills which are useful include the assertion skills needed for communicating effectively with parents and for collaborating with colleagues. These include techniques for giving constructive feedback, making and refusing requests, handling criticism and for problem solving.

SUMMARY AND CONCLUSIONS

Education Acts from 1980 to 1993 have gradually increased the rights of parents who have children with SEN to the extent that it is now imperative for schools to work closely with parents. A model which can be used to guide the practice of parental involvement and the steps involved in developing a school policy on involving parents have been described in order to help schools develop effective working relationships with parents. Suggestions have been provided on how to facilitate parental involvement in assessments and reviews, since this is now mandated by the Code of Practice. Finally, the attitudes, skills and knowledge needed in order to work effectively with parents were outlined. The interpersonal skills needed by SEN co-ordinators are discussed in more detail in the following chapter.

- statement of guiding principle of partnership between parents and teachers;

- statement of open-door policy regarding parents;

- procedures for establishing two-way communication between home and school;

- arrangements for recording and acting on concerns raised by parents;

- procedures for involving parents when a concern is first raised within the school;

- arrangomonto for optimising parent involvement in assessments and reviews of progress;

- procedures for ensuring that parents are kept informed about school organisation;

- procedures for reporting to parents on their children's progress;

- availability of parent education, guidance and support;

- opportunities for parents to reinforce school programmes at home;

- opportunities for parents who wish to do voluntary work at the school;

- opportunities for parents to become involved in the work of PTA or Governors;

- availability of a parents' room.

Figure 6.2 Checklist of elements to include in school policy for parental involvement

CHAPTER SEVEN

Skills Needed for Working with Parents and Specialists

INTRODUCTION

The importance for teachers of developing effective working relationships with parents of children with SEN was highlighted in the last chapter. Teachers also need to liaise with various other professionals such as educational psychologists and peripatetic teachers. The importance of collaborating with such colleagues was emphasised in Chapter Four. In order to work effectively with parents and other professionals, teachers of children with SEN need to develop a high level of interpersonal communication skills. While teachers typically have excellent skills in the areas of verbal presentation, explanation and information giving, they generally have less well-developed skills in the areas of listening, counselling and assertiveness (Seligman, 1979). These three skill areas are particularly important for teachers working with parents of children with SEN and other professionals and therefore are the focus of this chapter, along with the skills involved in managing the stress created by what is becoming an increasingly demanding job.

Probably the most essential of the four sets of skills are the ones needed for effective listening. These include the skills of attentiveness, passive listening, paraphrasing and active listening. Assertion skills are important too, both for communicating with parents and for collaborating with colleagues. These include techniques for making and refusing requests, giving constructive feedback, handling criticism and problem solving. Teachers also need to have a level of counselling skills sufficient to cope with the everyday concerns of parents of children with SEN. Therefore, a problem-solving model of counselling is described which involves listening, understanding and action planning skills. In addition, since teachers of children with SEN in general and SEN co-ordinators in particular are experiencing increased demands resulting from the implementation of the Code of Practice it is considered that managing the stress associated with these roles is essential if they are to work effectively and avoid 'burning out'. The stress management strategies which are described in this chapter include ones which focus on inter-personal, personal, task-related and organisational responses to stress. The various interpersonal skills needed by teachers of children with SEN are described below, starting with the skills required for effective listening.

LISTENING SKILLS

The skills required for listening effectively to another person are outlined below and presented in more detail elsewhere (Hornby, 1994). The major components of listening are attentiveness, passive listening, paraphrasing and active listening.

Attentiveness

Effective listening requires a high level of attentiveness. This involves focusing one's physical attention on the person being listened to and includes several components (Egan, 1982):

1   It is important to maintain good eye contact. While speakers often avert their eyes to concentrate on what they are saying, good listeners keep looking at the speaker's face, both to communicate attentiveness and to pick up non-verbal clues about the person's feelings from their facial expression.
2   One should face the speaker squarely, since turning one's body away from the other person suggests a lack of attention .
3   An open posture should be adopted. This means that neither arms nor legs should be crossed since this gives an impression of being less open to what the other person is saying.
4   One should lean slightly towards the other person. This communicates close attention to what is being said, whereas leaning back suggests a lack of interest.
5   Avoid distracting body movements, such as fidgeting in one's seat, or even worse clicking a pen, or worst of all looking at one's watch.
6   A comfortable distance should be maintained between talker and listener. The most appropriate distance varies from culture to culture and from person to person. Being too close could be embarrassing while sitting too

far apart may communicate disinterest.

7 It is important to remain relaxed while doing all of the above. It is more important to feel comfortable with the position adopted than to follow the above points slavishly.

8 A non-distracting environment should be created, that is, one in which you are not disturbed by a telephone ringing or someone coming in through the door.

Passive Listening

Passive listening involves using a high level of attentiveness combined with other skills. This involves the following:

1 The person should be invited to speak. For example, 'How can I help you?' or 'You seem upset. Would you like to talk about it?'

2 'Non-verbal grunts' let the speaker know that you are with them. For example, 'Go on', 'Right', 'Huh Huh'.

3 Avoid using communication blocks such as criticism (e.g. 'You shouldn't have done that'), reassurance (e.g. 'It'll be all right. You'll see') or advice (e.g. 'If I were you I would . . .').

4 Give the other person 100 per cent attention. This involves avoiding self-listening. That is, not going off into one's own thoughts while the other person is talking.

5 Open questions should be used for clarification or to encourage speakers to explore their concerns further. For example, 'What is it that you are most worried about?' or 'How do you mean?'

6 Attentive silence can be used in order to encourage speakers to open up. This requires listeners to pause for a few seconds after everything they say to encourage the other person to say more.

Paraphrasing

Paraphrasing is a skill which most people already use to some extent. When someone has told us something important and we want to be sure that we have understood correctly, we feed back the main points of the message to the person for his or her confirmation. This is a crude form of paraphrasing which is similar to that used by competent listeners.

An effective paraphrase has four components.

1 The paraphrase feeds back only the key points of the speaker's message.

2 Paraphrasing is concerned with the factual content of the speaker's

message, not with feelings.

3   An effective paraphrase is short and to the point. It is a summary of the speaker's key message, not a summary of everything said.

4   A paraphrase is stated in the listener's own words but in language which is familiar to the speaker (Bolton, 1979).

Paraphrases are used when there are natural breaks in the interaction, such as when speakers pause and look at the listener or when speakers inflect their voices at the end of a sentence, clearly wanting some response from the listener. At this point the listener feeds back the essence of the speaker's message and then waits for a response. When the paraphrase hits the mark speakers typically indicate that this is the case by saying, 'That's it' or 'Right' or 'Yes' or by some non-verbal means such as nodding their heads. If the paraphrase is not accurate or only partly accurate then the response will not be so positive and in most cases the speaker will correct the listener. In so doing speakers will also be clarifying for themselves exactly what is meant, so the paraphrase will still have been of value (Brammer, 1993).

Active Listening

Active listening is generally understood to be, *trying to understand what the person is feeling and what the key message is in what they are saying. Then putting this understanding into your own words and feeding it back to the person* (Gordon, 1970). Thus, active listening involves the listener being actively engaged in clarifying the thoughts and feelings of the person they are with. It builds on attentiveness, passive listening and paraphrasing in that the main aspects of what is being communicated are reflected back to the person. This is done to provide a kind of 'sounding board' to facilitate exploration and clarification of the person's concerns or ideas.

Gordon (1970) suggested that certain attitudes are essential pre-requisites to active listening. These are:

* the listener must really want to hear what the other person has to say;
* the listener must sincerely want to help the other person with his or her concern;
* the listener must be able to respect the other person's feelings or values even though they conflict with his or her own;
* the listener must have faith in the other person's ability to work through and solve his or her own problems;
* the listener must realise that feelings are transitory and not be afraid when people express strong feelings such as anger or sadness;
* the listener must accept that other people will have very different opinions, attitudes and values to themselves.

The process of active listening involves reflecting both thoughts and feelings back to the speaker. The speaker's key feeling is fed back along with the apparent reason for the feeling. When teachers are learning how to use active listening it is useful to have a set formula to follow. The formula, 'You feel ... because ...' is typically used. For example:

- 'You *feel* frustrated *because* you haven't finished the job.'
- 'You *feel* delighted *because* she has done so well.'

When teachers gain confidence in their use of active listening the formula is no longer needed and thoughts and feelings can be reflected back in a more natural way. For example:

- 'You *are* angry *about* the way you were treated.'
- '*You're* sad *that* it has come to an end.'
- 'You *were* pleased *with* the result.'
- 'You *were* annoyed *by* her manner.'

However, active listening involves much more than simply using this formula. It requires the listener to set aside his or her own perspective in order to understand what the other person is experiencing. It therefore involves being aware of how things are said, the expressions and gestures used and, most importantly, of hearing what is not said but which lies behind what is said. The real art in active listening is in feeding this awareness back to the person accurately and sensitively. This, of course, is very difficult, but the beauty of active listening is that you don't have to be completely right to be helpful. An active listening response which is a little off the mark typically gets the person who is talking to clarify his or her thoughts and feelings further. However, active listening responses which are way off the mark suggest to the speaker that the other person isn't listening and therefore act as blocks to communication.

COUNSELLING SKILLS

'Being a good listener is often not enough. Parents need help in specifying their problems and in establishing strategies to deal with those problems' (Kroth, 1985, p. 127). As suggested by this quotation, what is needed by teachers who work with parents of children with SEN is a broader model of helping which includes listening but which provides for going beyond this when circumstances demand it. The counselling model which is proposed for use with parents is based on a general approach to counselling which can be used with children and adults in a wide variety of situations. The model involves a 3-stage approach to counselling with stages of *listening, understanding* and *action planning*. It is a problem-solving approach to counselling adapted from previous models by Egan (1982) and Allan and Nairne (1984) and is described in more detail elsewhere (Hornby, 1994).

There are times when parents of children with SEN would benefit from counselling. However, the majority of parents will not ask for counselling directly, but will typically go to teachers with concerns about their children. Parents of children with SEN are much more likely to be willing to talk about their concerns with someone who is working directly with their child, such as a therapist or teacher, than with a professional counsellor who they do not know. If teachers use listening skills with parents then if they have any concerns these will emerge. Teachers should then be able to help by providing 'first aid' counselling and being prepared to refer parents on for more intensive help when necessary. What teachers need, therefore, is a 'first aid' counselling model which is practical, simple to learn and easy to use. A summary of the model proposed is presented in Figure 7.1. The rationale for using such a model is based on the idea that the majority of problems, concerns or ideas which parents bring to counselling can be dealt with by taking them through the 3 stages of the model in order to help them find the solution that best suits their situation. First of all, the teacher uses the skills of *listening*, which were discussed above, to establish a working relationship with parents, to help them open up and to help them explore any concerns or ideas they have.

Next, the teacher uses the skills of *understanding* in order to help parents get a clearer picture of their concerns or ideas, develop new perspectives on their situation, and suggest possible goals for change. Summarising is used in order to help parents clarify their major concerns or ideas. Parents are also given feedback on any themes which occur in what they are saying. Parents are then helped to develop new perspectives on their situations perhaps by teachers sharing from their experiences of working with children with SEN. Finally, to facilitate movement from stage 2 to stage 3, parents are helped to

STAGE	LISTENING	UNDERSTANDING	ACTION PLANNING
SKILLS	Attentiveness Passive listening	Summarising Identifying themes	Problem solving Developing action plans
	Paraphrasing Active listening	Changing perspectives Clarifying goals	Facilitating action Reviewing progress

Direction of movement in counselling process
→

Figure 7.1 Counselling model

develop realistic goals for solving their problems or implementing their ideas.

Then, the teacher moves on to *action planning*, in which problem-solving skills are used in order to help parents decide what, if anything, they want to do about their concern or idea. That is, to consider possible options for solving their problems or implementing their ideas. Parents are also helped to develop plans for action and assertively implement their plans. Finally, in subsequent sessions, parents are helped to review their progress in implementing their plans.

Possessing the skills required to use this simple 3-stage problem-solving model of counselling will contribute enormously to the ability of teachers to establish a productive partnership with parents. Many of the skills required for the third stage of the model are discussed in the following section on assertion skills.

ASSERTION SKILLS

Assertiveness involves being able to stand up for one's own rights while respecting the rights of others; being able to communicate one's ideas, concerns and needs directly, persistently and diplomatically; being able to express both positive and negative feelings with openness and honesty; and, being able to choose how to react to situations from a range of options.

Teachers need assertion skills both for working with parents and for collaborating with other professionals. Teachers will need to make and refuse requests and will have to deal with criticism and aggression from time to time. They will also need to be able to give constructive feedback to parents as well as colleagues. Finally, they will need to be able to help both parents and colleagues to resolve conflicts and solve problems. The skills involved in these situations are outlined below and are discussed in more detail elsewhere (Hornby, 1994).

Refusing a Request

Teachers will sometimes receive requests from parents or colleagues which they think they shouldn't agree to but feel unable to turn down. People have difficulty saying 'no' for several reasons, especially due to the fear that it will damage their relationship with the other person. The alternative to agreeing to requests you would rather turn down is to use acceptable ways of saying 'no', several of which are listed below.

• *The explained 'no'*. When you have a genuine reason for the refusal you can say 'no', explain why you are turning down the request, and give a brief apology. For example, 'No, I'm sorry, I can't make it because I'm already booked for that day.'

- *The postponed 'no'*. In this refusal you explain that you can't comply with the request at present but may be able to in the future. For example, 'No, I'm sorry, I'm not able to take that on today, but I may be able to help you with it in the future.'
- *The delayed 'no'*. In this technique you ask for time to think it over. This gives you the opportunity to carefully consider whether you want to comply with the request and to work out exactly how you will say 'no'. For example, 'I'm busy right now and I'd like to give it some thought. Can I get back to you tomorrow?'
- *The listening 'no'*. In this refusal active listening skills are used to let other people know that you understand the reason for their request. The listening response is combined with a brief apology and a firm refusal. For example, 'Yes I understand your frustration about not being able to get the job done. I'm sorry, but I can't help you with it.'
- *The 'get back to me' 'no'*. This involves explaining the difficulties you have in complying with the request. Then suggesting that the person try elsewhere and if all else fails to come back to you and you'll see what you can do. For example, 'I'm booked up for the next two weeks so I suggest you try elsewhere. If you really get stuck I'll do my best to fit you in but I can't promise anything.'
- *The 'broken record' 'no'*. This is a form of refusal which is particularly useful for dealing with people who won't take 'no' for an answer. It involves making a brief statement of refusal to the other person, avoiding getting into discussion with them, and simply repeating the statement as many times as necessary (like a broken record) until the message gets across. For example, 'I'm sorry but I can't help you.' ... 'Yes, I can see your problem, but I'm sorry, I can't help you.' ... 'As I said, I'm sorry but I can't help you.' ... etc.

Making a Request

Teachers sometimes need to request various things from their colleagues and occasionally need to make requests of parents. So, being able to make requests effectively is important, especially since many people find it difficult to do. Manthei (1981) has provided some useful guidelines for making requests and these are outlined below.

- *State your request directly*. State your request firmly and clearly to the other person.

- *Say exactly what you want.* Be specific and precise about your requirements.
- *Focus on the positive.* Create an expectation of compliance with your request.
- *Answer only questions seeking clarification.* Don't allow yourself to be side-tracked.
- *Allow the person time to think about it.* Suggest you'll get back to them later.
- *Repeat the request.* Use the 'broken record' technique to restate the request.
- *Be prepared to compromise.* You are better off getting partial agreement than rejection.
- *Realise the other person has the right to refuse.* Respect the other person's rights.

Responding to Criticism

Holland and Ward (1990) have described a model which is useful in considering how to respond to criticism. The 4 steps of the model are outlined below.

- *Step 1: Listening to the criticism.* Listening skills are useful in clarifying the criticism. Open questions such as, 'How do you mean?' or 'Can you be more specific?' are helpful in finding out exactly what the criticism is aimed at.
- *Step 2: Deciding on the truth.* Before responding to the criticism its validity should be considered. It is often wise to take some time to think about this before responding. The criticism may be completely true, partly true or completely untrue.
- *Step 3: Responding assertively.* If you consider the criticism to be completely true then it is best to agree with the critic, make a brief apology and assure them you will correct the situation. For example, 'I'm sorry about not consulting you on this matter. I'll make sure it doesn't happen again.'

  If you consider the criticism is partly true then you should agree with the part considered to be valid, briefly apologise, and at the same time correct the part which is false. For example, 'Yes, I did make a mistake in that case and I regret that, but I don't accept that I'm making mistakes all the time these days. I make occasional errors like anyone else.'

  If you consider the criticism to be completely false then you should clearly reject it, tell the other person exactly how the criticism makes us feel, ask for an explanation of their comments and make an affirmative statement about yourself. For example, 'I don't agree that I was wrong in that case and am greatly offended by the suggestion. What grounds could you possibly have for making such a comment? I believe my relationships with pupils are excellent.'

- *Step 4: Letting go.* Decide to use what you have learned from the criticism and about the critic and move on. Of course, this is 'much easier said than done' but it is important not to let ourselves be deflected from our goals by what is, after all, just one person's opinion.

Dealing with Aggression

Occasionally teachers have to deal with aggressive behaviour from parents or colleagues. Kroth (1985) has provided some guidelines for what teachers should do and should not do in this situation. *Teachers should not*:

- argue with a person who is behaving aggressively;
- raise their voices or begin to shout;
- become defensive and feel they have to protect their position;
- attempt to minimise the concern which the other person is expressing;
- take responsibility for problems which are not of their making;
- make promises which they won't be able to fulfil.

All of these responses are ones which are commonly used by people confronted with aggression but they seldom work and are more likely to make the other person more aggressive. The following responses are far more likely to calm the other person down and lead to a constructive resolution of the situation. *Teachers should*:

- actively listen to the other person, reflecting back their thoughts and feelings in order to confirm that you are listening and to help you understand their perspective;
- speak softly, slowly and calmly;
- ask for clarification of any complaints which are vague;
- ask them what else is bothering them in order to exhaust their list of complaints;
- make a list of their concerns, show them the list and ask if it's correct and complete;
- use the techniques of problem solving, discussed below, to work through their list of concerns in order to resolve the problems or conflicts, starting with the one of highest priority to the other person.

Giving Constructive Feedback

Giving constructive feedback to others is an important skill for both our professional and personal lives. Whereas criticism is generally given without the intention of helping the other person, constructive feedback is aimed at helping them to function better. A model for providing constructive feedback which has been found extremely useful is one adapted from the DESC script popularised by Bower and Bower (1976). This is a technique which teachers find valuable in giving feedback to parents of children with SEN and also to their colleagues and which, in addition, parents find useful in handling difficulties with professionals. DESC stands for: describe; express; specify; and consequences. The 4 steps involved in using the modified DESC script are described below.

1   *Describe*. Describe the behaviour of concern in the most specific and objective terms possible. For example, 'When you change a child's programme without consulting me . . .'
2   *Express or explain*. Either express your feelings about this behaviour or explain the difficulties it causes for you, or do both, calmly and positively, without blaming or judging the other person, or 'putting them down'. For example, '. . . I get very annoyed (*express*) because we are supposed to work together on such things' (*explain*).
3   *Specify*. Specify the exact change in behaviour required of the other person. For example, '. . . So, in future, will you make sure you consult me before making such changes . . .'
4   *Consequences*. The consequences which are likely to result from the other person complying with the request are stated. The benefits for both people are stated along with any concessions which you are willing to make. For example, '. . . I would be happy to discuss such changes at times convenient to you and feel sure that we'd work more effectively that way.' If the other person is not willing to comply, then the modified DESC script should be repeated including the negative consequences for the person of not complying with the request. For example, '. . . If you do not consult me as I suggest then I will have to insist on having regular formal meetings with you.'

Preparation and delivery.   Although the modified DESC script is simple enough to be thought up and delivered on the spot it is usually best to write it out beforehand. It is then possible to make sure that the wording is suitable and also to rehearse it with a third person in order to get feedback on it. It can then be decided when, where and how it will be delivered.

Problem Solving and Conflict Resolution

Often teachers find that their opinions differ from those of parents or their colleagues. Where there is a serious conflict of opinions or needs it can lead to a deterioration in relationships unless these difficulties are resolved. Bolton (1979) has proposed a model for collaboration in solving problems or resolving conflicts which is useful in this situation. The 6 steps of the model are described below.

1 *Define problem from each person's perspective.* This involves the use of active listening in order to clarify the other person's opinions and needs and, if possible, to understand the reasons for these. It also involves stating one's own case assertively. This is a key element of the model and may take up half of the total time required for the process.
2 *Brainstorming possible solutions.* Once both persons' views are understood, brainstorming can be used to seek solutions which meet both sets of needs. First, as many potential solutions as possible should be listed, without attempting to evaluate or clarify any of them. Wild ideas should be included as these often spark off more creative solutions. Then, each other's ideas should be expanded on and clarified.
3 *Select solutions which meet both party's needs.* A choice is then made from the list of potential solutions of the one which best meets the needs of both parties. This will probably involve discussing the relative merits of several solutions in meeting each other's needs.
4 *Plan who will do what, where and by when.* It may be useful to make a written note of the decision about what each party will do, where it will be done and when it will be completed.
5 *Implement the plan.* It is clearly important that each party should attempt to follow the agreement closely in implementing the plan.
6 *Evaluate the process and the solution.* An essential part of the problem-solving process is to agree a time when both parties can meet to evaluate how well the solution is meeting each of their needs.

STRESS MANAGEMENT SKILLS

The Need for Managing Stress

The purpose of this section is to help teachers who work with children with SEN to manage stress more effectively and thereby avoid 'burning out'. These teachers will then be able to pass on stress management techniques to their colleagues and to the parents of children with SEN with whom they work. In the first part of this section, some facts about stress and burnout are discussed and the importance of identifying the symptoms of too much stress is emphasised. Then, a range of strategies for stress management are presented. These include strategies which focus on personal, interpersonal, task-related and organisational factors which need to be addressed in order to effectively manage stress.

Effects of Stress

Stress can manifest itself in a wide variety of ways. When people are under severe stress it tends to first affect any areas of physical or psychological weakness which a person has. For some people the signs of too much stress may be problems with their stomach, for others it is difficulty in sleeping at night. A few people experience unusual and sometimes frightening physical symptoms such as numbness in a limb. The symptoms of burnout include feeling tense, exhausted or depressed. People at risk of burning out may develop negative attitudes towards other people, become generally cynical or experience little feeling of accomplishment in their jobs or personal lives. They may frequently be ill, have a lot of time off work, and increase their use of drugs such as alcohol and tobacco. Experiencing these symptoms of burnout on a long-term basis can have serious consequences for a person's psychological and physiological health. There are also substantial negative effects on organisations such as schools due to staff suffering the effects of burnout, including excessive absenteeism, lower overall morale among staff and less effective teaching and administration. Therefore, it is important, both for schools and for individual teachers, to manage stress appropriately and thereby avoid the debilitating effects of burnout. The first step in this is for teachers to recognise the early signs of burnout and to employ suitable strategies to manage the stress in their lives.

Stress Management Strategies

People are very different in the ways they cope with high levels of stress. What works for some people does not work for others. Therefore, a wide range of strategies for coping with stress are outlined below, from which teachers can choose the specific techniques most suited to themselves. However, it is important to address each of the personal, interpersonal, task-related and organisational aspects of stress, including time management, in order to avoid the negative effects which stress can have on our lives.

Interpersonal strategies

For teachers of children with SEN, the majority of the stress they experience at work results from their relationships with colleagues within the school and the other professionals with whom they work. Therefore, it is essential that teachers develop the skills of communicating assertively with their colleagues in order to reduce the stress levels in their interpersonal relationships. Full use should be made of the assertion skills discussed earlier in this chapter including: saying 'no' when you need to; giving constructive feedback; and techniques for dealing with criticism or aggression.

Another strategy for reducing stress levels which is in the interpersonal domain is related to how personal concerns are dealt with. Talking over problems with other people often helps to reduce stress. Sharing concerns is particularly useful when the other person has experienced similar problems, since this generates a feeling of 'being in the same boat' which is widely acknowledged to be therapeutic (Yalom, 1985). Having a network of colleagues, friends and family members who can provide support and a listening ear when stress levels get too high is tremendously valuable. Teachers should therefore be continually aware of maintaining, and if possible expanding, their support network, so that in times of need there will be people available to provide support.

Sometimes the effects of stress are so debilitating that help from a professional counsellor would be beneficial, but this is probably the type of help which is most difficult for the majority of people to accept. People of British descent tend to think that they must be 'dangling from the light-shade' before needing professional counselling. An example of just how helpful stress counselling can be was provided by a teacher who was having frightening sensations of feeling heavier and fatter after experiencing a distressing incident with a pupil and a car accident within a short period of time. A 10-minute counselling session was sufficient to help her to get rid of these sensations, using a simple technique which involved her focusing her complete attention on these sensations.

Emotional strategies

Useful skills for coping with stress are those which are based on *centring* (Laurie and Tucker, 1982), *breathing* (Madders, 1979) and *relaxation techniques* (Cautela and Groden, 1978). *Hypnotism*, *massage* and various forms of *meditation*, including yoga, involve combinations of these three types of technique and have been used for centuries to help people cope with stress. Techniques which have become popular more recently for facilitating relaxation are *guided fantasy* and *progressive relaxation*. In guided fantasy people are encouraged to close their eyes and imagine themselves in some relaxing situation, such as having a long hot bath, lying on a beach, drifting down the river on a boat, or going for a stroll in the countryside. In progressive relaxation people learn to tense and relax the various muscle groups throughout the body, from head to toe, so that they become more aware of any tension in the body and are able to relax all these muscle groups in order to achieve total relaxation. These techniques are described in detail elsewhere (Hall and Hall, 1988).

Cognitive strategies

It has been shown that our emotional and physiological reactions to events are affected by the way we perceive these events (Meichenbaum, 1985). More specifically, it is the things we tell ourselves about the way we and others should act that often creates unnecessary stress. Mills (1982) points out that people tend to have unconscious rules about the way they and others ought to behave. For example, they believe such things as, 'I must never make a mistake' or 'Other people should always think highly of me.'

These unspoken rules create high levels of stress when we try to live up to them, or expect others to. Therefore, as Mills suggests, we need to make ourselves aware of our unconscious rules, challenge the thinking that accompanies them and revise them to produce less stressful messages such as, 'I would rather not make any mistakes but if I do it just shows that I'm human' or 'I like others to think well of me but realise that some won't and I can live with that.'

In addition to changing unconscious rules it is also useful to change any negative, stress-producing thoughts to positive, calming ones (Meichenbaum, 1985). For example: 'Stay calm. You can handle this well as long as you don't lose your temper' or 'Worrying about it will do no good. Whatever happens you can handle it.' By using such positive self-statements to counteract any negative thoughts, stress levels can be considerably reduced.

Another way to reduce stress is through visualisation (Gawain, 1982). Developing the art of positive visualisation has been shown to have therapeutic effects in both personal and professional situations (Shaw, Bensky and Dixon, 1981). Visualising oneself feeling relaxed in situations which normally create tension can be helpful, as can visualising oneself achieving a desired goal.

Finally, keeping a healthy sense of humour is a powerful strategy for managing stress. Being able to see the funny side of one's difficulties is a good way to keep them in perspective.

Physical strategies

Taking care of oneself physically is an essential aspect of stress management. Getting adequate sleep and rest is very important. Having a healthy diet, eating regular meals and avoiding the abuse of drugs such as alcohol, tobacco, tea and coffee are other important aspects of effective stress management (Madders, 1979). A common response to high levels of stress is to eat more which can lead to becoming overweight. Of course, it is best not to use food for gratification when under stress but if you can't avoid doing this sometimes then it is important to make sure that you exercise regularly. Participating in vigorous exercise at least three times a week is one of the best ways to avoid the negative effects of stress. Some people like to join a gym or health club and have an organised exercise programme, others prefer regular involvement in sports such as tennis, badminton, bowling or golf. However, the best exercises for the body as a whole are thought to be swimming and brisk walking. Ideally, exercise should be built into your daily routine, for example, by walking to work or having a lunch time jog every day.

Another important aspect of stress management is the need for a change of environment from time to time. Mills (1982) suggests getting completely away from home and work environments on vacation at least once a year and also taking some weekends off to 'get away from it all'. It's also important to have changes of scene built into one's weekly routine perhaps through involvement in a club or with a hobby which is unrelated to teaching.

Organisational strategies

Much of the stress which teachers experience is caused by organisational factors at their school, such as poor communication between the management team and staff or an incompetent head of department. Of course, the most effective long-time strategy to deal with such difficulties can be to bring about constructive change by becoming as involved as possible in the management of the school. However, such organisational factors are often ones which are difficult for individuals to change without expending enormous amounts of energy, so in addition, it is necessary to adopt specific strategies to manage these work-related stressors.

One way of reducing stress at school is to develop collaborative working relationships with colleagues who are open to this. Conducting co-operative ventures with individuals or small groups of colleagues encourages teamwork and tends to increase everyone's effectiveness (Covey, 1989). Additionally, it is sometimes possible to get together a small group of colleagues into a support group. This can be a fairly formal group which could perhaps meet at lunch times, or it can be quite informal with a few people getting together over a drink once a week. Either way, this can be very supportive and is a useful strategy for reducing stress levels.

Another useful strategy is to keep a clear distinction between work and home by leaving all incomplete work at school rather than bringing it home.

It is usually better, if something has to be finished, to stay a little longer at work to get it done rather than bringing it home and having it ruin your evening or weekend.

Also important in controlling work-related stress is not losing sight of one's career aspirations. Seeing the current job as a step on the way to where one wants to be in a few years' time is a way of keeping problems in perspective. Losoncy (1982) suggests that one should continually attend to self-promotion activities, that is, always allocating some work time to developing something that will facilitate movement towards career goals.

Time management

A key component of coping with stress for busy people, which is task related, is managing time as efficiently as possible. Much has been written about this topic in recent years (Black, 1987; Ferner, 1980; Fontana, 1993; Turla and Hawkins, 1985). According to this literature the essential elements of time management are establishing priorities and carefully planning the use of your time.

Other important aspects of time management include: delegating as many tasks as possible; saying 'no' to new responsibilities you don't want to take on; and making daily lists of jobs to be done. One strategy which is particularly useful is forcing oneself to handle a particular piece of paper once only, if at all possible. Most memos and letters can be dealt with on the spot, either by writing a note back on the bottom or by perusing them before putting them in the waste-basket. Only things which can't be dealt with immediately should be left for later attention.

Another important strategy is not wasting time in meetings. Meetings should be kept short and to the point with a maximum of an hour allotted to them. The rationale for this is that an efficiently run meeting should be over in an hour with any items needing longer consideration being delegated to an individual or sub-committee to look into and report back to the next meeting.

A further aspect of time management is ensuring that the most intellectually demanding tasks are done early in the day when one is fresh. More mundane tasks can be assigned to later in the day.

A common problem is that people often procrastinate on tasks because they seem so overwhelming when all that needs to be done is considered. In this situation it is generally useful to do a simple 'task analysis', that is, break the task down into manageable components and tackle it step by step. Focusing on one step at a time helps prevent being overwhelmed by the enormity of the task. 'Grandma's rule' can also be a useful strategy for dealing with procrastination, whereby some treat or favoured activity is made contingent on getting a certain task completed.

SUMMARY AND CONCLUSIONS

It has been argued that teachers in general, and SEN co-ordinators in particular, will need to have highly developed interpersonal skills in order to effectively work with parents, collaborate with colleagues and liaise with outside specialists. The most important set of skills are considered to be listening skills, including paraphrasing and active listening. Assertion skills are also regarded as being important skills for SEN co-ordinators to possess. The skills involved in using a simple 3-stage model of counselling build on the listening and assertion skills already described. Finally, stress management skills, including those of time management, are outlined in order to help SEN co-ordinators manage the stress associated with the increased demands of the Code of Practice.

CHAPTER EIGHT

OFSTED Inspection and SEN

INTRODUCTION

OFSTED inspection is an aspect of school life which is viewed with considerable apprehension by many teachers. Inspectors are there to check that the school has all the necessary policy documents and that what the school says is happening in those documents is actually happening. They will also be monitoring the quality of teaching and ensuring that the school is complying with educational legislation. All this is very clearly set out in the OFSTED Inspection Manual (1993), both in the Framework and the Technical Papers.

A complete section is devoted to SEN provision within the manual. If these sections are read in conjunction with the Code of Practice it can be seen that where a school is operating the Code effectively, it will also be meeting the OFSTED inspection criteria.

Schools can also prepare themselves for an inspection by seeking information from and giving information to the chief inspector. A checklist of the kind of questions to ask and the information that should be made available is given in Figure 8.1. Questions should be asked through the head teacher at the initial meeting with the chief inspector. Whether information should be provided prior to, or at, the inspectorial team's arrival in the school should be negotiated with the chief inspector.

The OFSTED Inspection Manual provides information concerning what the inspectors are looking for and what evidence they will use to judge how effectively the provision is made. Therefore this information can be used to provide guidelines for SEN policy and practice within schools. These guidelines are described in the remainder of this chapter.

Prior to the inspectors' arrival in the school it may be helpful to seek and provide specific information. Here is a checklist to follow:

- *Ask* for copies of the inspectors' CVs, either through the head at the initial meeting with the chief inspector or through the parents' meeting. It will be helpful to find out if any of the inspectors have SEN experience or qualifications.
- *Provide* a copy of the school's SEN policy ensuring that it is up to date and meets legal requirements.
- *Provide* a copy of the school's SEN register.
- *Provide* details of screening procedures and a copy of the results.
- *Provide* a copy of the timetables for support work and of the SEN department staff.
- *Provide* an inventory of specialist equipment.
- *Provide* details of the SEN budget.
- *Provide* a list of special needs staff, their qualifications, roles and responsibilities.

Even if you do not provide these prior to the inspection, have them readily available when the inspectors are in the school.

Figure 8.1 SEN co-ordinators and OFSTED inspection (information checklist)

Evaluation Criteria

The provision which a school makes will be judged by the extent to which it enables pupils with SEN to make the greatest progress possible. It is therefore necessary for the school to be able to provide evidence of the progress made. This could be achieved through a variety of means, including progress through National Curriculum levels of attainment, standardised test results, internal school test results and evidence accumulated through an individual pupil's portfolio of work.

The school's SEN provision will also be judged by the access SEN pupils have to a broad and balanced curriculum, which includes the subjects of the National Curriculum (except where modification or disapplication applies to a pupil), religious education and other curricular provision such as personal and social education or careers guidance.

Sources of Evidence

The Framework section of the Inspection manual identifies *fourteen* aspects of the school's SEN provision which will be used to provide evidence to inform the inspection. These are outlined below.

1 *Pupil achievement*. The standards of achievement of individual pupils could, for example, include the results of any screening test procedures operated by the school, pupil profiles produced through either standardised tests or individual diagnostic assessments, exam results, National Curriculum levels of attainment or portfolios of work produced.

2 *Support for SEN*. The level and effectiveness of the support provided for pupils with SEN in relation to the numbers of these pupils (including those with statements) within the school. This will include matters like the organisation and deployment of the SEN budget, staffing, resources and materials.

3 *SEN policy*. The clarity of the school's SEN policy and its effectiveness in enabling the school to respond to the needs of pupils and parents. It is important to ensure that roles, responsibilities, procedures, targets and the school's policy in relation to the LEA's SEN policy are clearly identified and addressed.

4 *Monitoring of funding*. The procedures that are adopted for monitoring the funding available for SEN pupils and how it is spent.

5 *Statements of SEN*. The school has to demonstrate that it is fulfilling the requirements identified on individual pupils' statements of special educational needs. This includes ensuring that the relevant information on statements is communicated to the staff concerned and that all teachers

who have a teaching role with a pupil who is the subject of a statement fulfil the requirements of that statement. It is important to remember that an inspector will track a statemented pupil for at least half a day.

6 *National Curriculum arrangements.* Arrangements that are made to ensure appropriate access to, modification of or disapplication from the National Curriculum where necessary. Any such modifications or disapplications must be clearly identified and suitable alternatives put in place. Consideration must be given to whether withdrawal arrangements of pupils for any reason during the school day causes undue disruption of NC requirements.

7 *Teaching arrangements.* The appropriateness and effectiveness of the teaching arrangements made for pupils with SEN. Consideration will be given to the organisational arrangements for teaching such as the use of support teaching and/or withdrawal arrangements for individual or small group tuition.

8 *Staffing allocations.* The provision of staff to meet SEN within the school. This will include both the provision made from within the school establishment and its deployment and the use of specialists from outside the school.

9 *Support teachers and services.* The use that is made of support teachers and outside specialists, both in terms of pupil access to such provision and the deployment within the school, for pupils with SEN.

10 *Integration.* The extent to which pupils are integrated into the school and the appropriateness of such arrangements. This will include whether the integration model used is total, functional or social and how effective it is for both SEN pupils and their peers.

11 *Identification procedures.* The selection and use of screening and assessment procedures and the information that is obtained as a result.

12 *Accommodation and resources.* The availability of specialist accommodation and resources and the extent to which modifications have been made to assist physical access to the site and buildings for groups with SEN.

13 *Consultation arrangements – school.* The arrangements that are made to enable effective discussions with staff, pupils and parents to take place.

14 *Consultation arrangements – external agencies.* The arrangements made for and the extent of discussions with medical, paramedical and nursing specialists, psychologists and other outside specialists.

EVALUATION CRITERIA:
KEY QUESTIONS

In the Technical Papers section, the OFSTED Manual provides a list of *nine* key questions which are particularly relevant to SEN provision. Each key question is accompanied by a checklist of related issues that the inspectors will be using to evaluate the school's provision for pupils with SEN. These are summarised below.

1 *Standards of achievement*

'Are The Standards Achieved Appropriate To The Pupil's Abilities?' (OFSTED, 1993, Technical Papers, p. 63).
The inspector will be looking to see if the work produced matches the lesson's stated aims and objectives and if the achievements of the pupils match the written assessment of their ability. Inspectors will be looking for evidence which shows that the standards achieved match the individual objectives for each pupil and the teacher's knowledge of the pupil. They will also be looking at the quality of the pupil's past work in order to evaluate progress made.

2 *Quality of learning*

'Do Pupils Demonstrate A Satisfactory Level Of Competence As Learners?' (OFSTED, 1993, Technical Papers, p. 63).

1 *Learning skills*. In order to assess the pupils' learning skills the inspectors will need to know pupils' levels of ability. They will be assessing whether pupils have a positive attitude to work and whether they pay sufficient attention in lessons. In connection with this they will be looking to see if pupils remain involved with their work during the lesson and if they are able to participate fully and appropriately. Learning styles will also be considered to see whether pupils are able to work collaboratively or independently when necessary and evidence of pupils taking responsibility for their own learning. Finally, inspectors will be checking whether pupils are able and willing to evaluate the quality of their work.
2 *Learning outcomes*. The inspectors will be looking to see if pupils achieve the required objectives by using different routes. Pupils will need to demonstrate that they have made progress in knowledge, understanding and skills either orally or practically or both and that they can apply the knowledge and skills they have learned in new situations. Further evidence will include whether pupils understand the purpose of what they are learning and its applications and whether they choose appropriate resources in order to complete tasks.

3 Quality of teaching

'Does The Teaching Enable Pupils With SEN To Make Optimum Progress In The Subjects Of The Curriculum?' (OFSTED, 1993, Technical Papers, p. 65).

1 *Planning*. The inspectors are interested in lesson content to see if it is appropriate and relevant to the needs of all pupils in the class. It will be important to show that lessons are carefully planned to take account of the needs of pupils with SEN. The lesson plan should incorporate the contributions of other professionals where appropriate.
2 *Strategies*. The inspectors are assessing the teaching methods that are used, looking for variety, appropriateness and effectiveness.
3 *Teaching and learning*. The focus for this is the need to make work sufficiently challenging for all pupils whilst ensuring that the pace of the work is appropriate. It is important to ensure that expectations for the outcomes of learning tasks are also appropriate. There is a need to demonstrate positive interactions between teachers and pupils with SEN.
4 *Staff deployment*. The school needs to demonstrate that support staff are deployed effectively and efficiently to meet identified needs.

4 Assessment, recording and reporting

'Do The School's Arrangements For Assessment And Recording Enable It To Identify And Meet Individual Learning Needs, And To Record And Monitor Progress In Learning? Do Arrangements for Reporting Meet Statutory Requirements?' (OFSTED, 1993, Technical Papers, p. 66).

1 *Assessment*. This section is particularly concerned with the way in which pupils with SEN are identified including the use made of pre-school or transfer information to help inform the identification process. It is also important to show that assessment and recording procedures arise out of curriculum developments and that the assessment methods used are appropriate for pupils with a wide range of abilities. The assessment procedures should also clarify and diagnose individual needs and should involve all staff who teach pupils with SEN. Having identified SEN pupils, the inspectors will be looking at the ways in which such information is disseminated to the rest of the staff and whether this assessment data informs teachers' planning.
2 *Recording*. It is important to ensure that records for pupils with SEN follow the whole-school policy and that there is appropriate co-ordination of SEN and mainstream records. This is discussed in greater detail in Chapters Three and Four.
3 *Reporting*. Reports on pupils with SEN should celebrate their achieve-

ments across the curriculum, including achievements in personal and social education and vocational education as well as conforming to whole-school reporting policy.

4 *Management of procedures for pupils with statements.* Arrangements made for the annual review of a statement must meet the statutory requirements and involve the pupil where appropriate, as discussed in Chapters Five and Six. If there are any modifications or disapplications made to any of the subjects in the National Curriculum these must be recorded on the statement.

5 The Curriculum

'Do The Content, Organisation, Planning And Implementation Of The Curriculum For Pupils With SEN Secure The Statutory Individual Entitlement?' (OFSTED, 1993, Technical Papers, p. 67).

1 *Content.* The inspectors are interested in assessing whether the curriculum provided for pupils with SEN is broad, balanced and relevant to their needs. Where appropriate individual programmes of work should be in operation and all pupils should enjoy equal access to the whole curriculum. Inspectors will be looking to see how often subjects, parts of subjects, attainment targets or assessment arrangements are modified or disapplied for pupils with SEN.

2 *Planning.* Schemes of work should reflect the needs of individual pupils and procedures to protect pupils' entitlement must be followed (as defined in Education Reform Act 1988, sections 17–19). Planning for the delivery of the National Curriculum should provide a reasonable amount of time for each subject as recommended.

3 *Organisation.* This is concerned particularly with arrangements to integrate pupils as fully as possible into ordinary classes or subject groups and to monitor and evaluate those arrangements to ensure that the pupils' needs, and those of their peers without SEN, are met effectively. It also has to be shown that the support that is provided for pupils with SEN in ordinary classes is sufficient to ensure appropriate access to the curriculum. Where pupils with SEN are integrated into mainstream classes, the arrangements for withdrawal work or for support teaching or therapy must avoid undue disruption of pupils' work and their entitlement to the National Curriculum. Where there is withdrawal teaching, the additional support provided and the class work should be co-ordinated. The pupil should be fully involved in decisions about the provision that is made to meet his or her needs and its evaluation.

6 Management and administration

'Do The School's Policies Facilitate the Identification, Assessment, Provision And Review Of Pupils With SEN And Enable Governors, Head And Staff To Evaluate The Effectiveness And Efficiency Of Arrangements?' (OFSTED, 1993, Technical Papers, p. 68).

The school's policy statement on the curriculum should include all necessary references to the requirements of pupils with SEN. There must be a named governor and member of the senior management team who have a designated responsibility for SEN. Departmental policies should reflect the school's SEN policy and there should be identifiable methods by which the policies are implemented, monitored and evaluated to ensure access to a balanced, broadly based curriculum – including the National Curriculum and religious education – is achieved. Planning and practice should involve other agencies or support provision from outside the school to meet individual needs. The SEN co-ordinator should be involved in policy and budget discussions and the governors and the LEA informed appropriately concerning National Curriculum modifications and disapplications.

7 Resources and their management

'Are There Sufficient, Appropriate Members Of Staff Deployed To Provide The Levels And Nature Of Learning Support That Pupils Need In Order To Enjoy Full Access To The Curriculum?' (OFSTED, 1993, Technical Papers, p. 69).

1   *Teaching and non-teaching staff.*
    (a) *Teachers.* Inspectors will be looking at the staffing levels to ascertain if these are sufficient to meet the needs of SEN pupils. They will be considering whether the SEN co-ordinator has appropriate status, qualifications and expertise and is a member of policy-making groups. They will be interested in whether subject departments in secondary schools have a designated teacher with responsibility for SEN and whether the SEN co-ordinator liaises with these teachers, and other members of staff, on a regular basis. An important consideration is the availability of suitable specialist in-service training on SEN to all the staff in the school. Deployment of staff is also looked at to see if SEN pupils and lower-ability groups have access to teachers who are as experienced and well qualified as those of mainstream groups. The work of support staff (teachers, special support assistants and any others involved) should be planned and co-ordinated with subject and class teachers.
    (b) *Special Support Assistants (SSA).* As with teaching staff, the inspectors are concerned with the effective and efficient employment of

SSAs in order to enhance pupils' learning. This has to be done without compromising the development of the individual pupil's independence. Where SSAs are employed, the numbers should reflect the advice given in DES Circular 11/90. Appropriate training should be provided for SSAs.

(c) *Supporting services*. The external supporting services used should be suitable to cater for the range of SEN identified and the work of any services involved planned with subject and class teachers. Outside specialists should be used efficiently and effectively (see Chapter Four).

2 *Resources for learning*. 'Do The Resources Provided For Pupils With SEN Enable Them To Gain Full Access To The Whole Curriculum?' (OFSTED, 1993, Technical Papers, p. 70).

Equipment and differentiated materials should be available in classes and subject departments to support the learning of pupils with SEN. Also, suitable specialist equipment should be available to pupils with physical or sensory disabilities. Pupils with SEN should have the same access to resources as other pupils. It is important to have facilities for the testing of specialist resources like hearing aids and for such things as recharging the batteries. All specialist equipment should be stored securely and its use should be monitored and recorded. Inspectors will also be checking whether staff have sufficient expertise to ensure that resources are used to the best advantage including the use of information technology. Pupils with SEN should have regular access to any library and resource facilities.

3 *Accommodation*. 'Does The Site, Including Premises And Grounds, Allow Full And Equal Access To The Curriculum For Pupils With SEN? Where Pupils Are Withdrawn For Support Teaching Is The Accommodation Provided Of Equal Quality To That Provided For Other Pupils?' (OFSTED, 1993, Technical Papers, p. 70).

The inspectors will be concerned with the working and learning environment provided for pupils with SEN in such terms as hygiene, health and safety, and building regulations. Accommodation provided for SEN pupils should be integral to the school, have appropriate facilities for changing and toileting purposes and have adjustable furniture and work surfaces where necessary. The furniture that is available in such accommodation should be capable of being used flexibly in order to cater for both individual and small group tuition arrangements. There should also be adequate, secure storage facilities for specialist equipment and resources, as well as confidential records and information.

8 Pupils' welfare and guidance

'Is There Coherent Guidance For Meeting The Needs Of Pupils Who Need Learning Support?' (OFSTED, 1993, Technical Papers, p. 71).

The inspectors will be reviewing the arrangements for the identification and support of pupils with emotional and behavioural difficulties (EBD) and seeing if these are co-ordinated with other SEN arrangements. They will also be interested to find out to what extent pupils with SEN are integrated into general class groupings for pastoral and curriculum support.

9 Links with parents, agencies and other institutions

'Are The Contributions Of Parents And Of Staff Of Other Agencies Effectively Co-ordinated So That The Pupil Receives A Coherent Learning Programme?' (OFSTED, 1993, Technical Papers, p. 71).

Under this heading the inspectors will be moderating the extent to which parents are involved in decisions about the provision made to meet their child's needs. The extent of the child's involvement in such decisions will also be considered. Also under consideration will be the role played by medical and para-medical staff, and staff from other agencies in such discussions and decisions. Inspectors will also be concerned with the extent to which all these parties are involved in the monitoring and evaluation of provision made. It is important to show that such contributions fully inform the pupils' learning programmes. All these discussions should be noted in the school's records.

CONCLUSION

It may not be possible for schools to meet all these requirements immediately. However, if they know that they are failing in a particular area, it is best not to attempt to hide the fact and hope that the inspector will not notice. Admitting the deficiency and suggesting a timescale for making appropriate provision is a better strategy. This will show inspectors that the school is in the process of monitoring provision, identifying areas to be improved and issues to be addressed and, by so doing, allowing inspectors to temper any criticisms that they make. Further discussion of OFSTED inspections of SEN provisions can be found in several recent articles on the topic (Carpenter and Stoneham, 1994; Chorley, 1993; Landy, 1994; Stone, 1993).

Note that the 1994 amendment to the OFSTED Technical Papers on SEN provides almost identical guidance to that presented in the 1993 edition except that inspectors will also be expected to evaluate whether schools have paid 'reasonable regard' to the Code and whether teachers use individual programmes in line with the 'staged procedures' outlined in the Code.

CHAPTER NINE

Future Challenges for Meeting SEN in Mainstream Schools

INTRODUCTION

Since the Code of Practice was circulated in draft form in Ocotber 1993 many teachers and others concerned with children with SEN have expressed reservations about it. These reservations have mostly not been about the usefulness of the procedures suggested by the Code but about the practicability of implementing it in schools. This is because putting the Code into practice is likely to involve considerable extra work for all teachers concerned, particularly SEN co-ordinators. Also, the Government have made it clear that no additional money will be provided to schools or LEAs to implement the Code since it is considered that the existing resources which schools are given to cater for pupils with SEN should be sufficient. This has prompted some people to suggest that the Code is part of a cynical exercise by the Government to save money on children with SEN by placing more obligations on mainstream schools, thereby reducing the numbers of children obtaining statements of SEN and places in special schools.

The conflict between the requirements of the Code and the lack of resources being provided to implement it has led to a situation where many teachers are feeling resentful about having it imposed on them and are uncertain about how they will meet the heavy demands generated by the Code. This is very unfortunate since it detracts attention from the positive features of the Code and the potential benefits which it could bring about.

The rationale for producing the Code is rooted in the recent history of legislation concerning children with SEN. It is widely acknowledged that the strategies used to implement the 1981 Education Act did not bring about the desired changes in provision for pupils with SEN in mainstream schools which were envisaged by the Warnock Report (DES, 1978). For example, a survey of 100 secondary schools found that, in the decade following the Warnock Report, few of its major recommendations had resulted in significant changes in their SEN provision (Stakes and Hornby, 1994). Further support for this finding were provided by the HMI/Audit Commission report (DES, 1992) which stated that important aspects of the 1981 Education Act were not being satisfactorily implemented by schools and LEAs. No doubt this report provided some of the impetus for the Government deciding to use another approach to attempt to get schools and LEAs to adopt the principles espoused by the Warnock Report, that is, through publication of a code of practice. If the Code of Practice succeeds in bringing about the changes in provision for SEN intended by the Warnock committee then this will have been a major achievement which will be to the advantage of numerous children with SEN.

It certainly appears that having a code of practice for SEN whose implementation is to be monitored by OFSTED inspections is proving a powerful force for change within schools and LEAs. It has been noticeable how, in recent months, LEAs have been scrambling to put together guidance for schools on the implementation of the Code as well as running training courses for SEN co-ordinators. Further, many LEAs have been setting up parent partnership schemes whose primary purpose is to provide support for parents as their children with SEN are taken through the statutory assessment and statementing process. It has also been noticeable that many schools have advertised SEN co-ordinator posts in which they have referred to the increased demands made by the Code of Practice and offered up to four salary incentive points in recognition of the importance they now place on the role of the SEN co-ordinator within the school.

It therefore seems that the emergence of the Code of Practice has given provisions for SEN a high profile within mainstream schools. It could be that the publication of the Code has created a rare opportunity for teachers in this field to make significant improvements in provisions for children with SEN in primary and secondary schools. However, in order to make optimum use of this opportunity teachers concerned with SEN in mainstream schools, especially SEN co-ordinators, will have to address several challenges. These are discussed below.

Challenge 1: Establishing effective school-wide identification and assessment procedures

The importance placed on the identification and assessment of SEN by the Code is emphasised by the focus on these two aspects of SEN provision in its title. The identification of children who have special educational needs of one kind or another and the assessment of these needs are seen as key areas for schools to focus on when organising their SEN provision. In the past, schools have tended to have their own idiosyncratic procedures for identifying and assessing SEN. In many schools these have been excellent but in some they have been inadequate.

In light of the Code all schools need to review their practices with regard to the identification of SEN. This involves re-considering the screening procedures they use for children on entry to the school and the mechanisms by which teachers who, during the year, identify children who are experiencing difficulties.

The Code stresses the importance of taking into account discrepancies between children's attainments and realistic expectations of their performance by parents, teachers and other professionals such as educational psychologists. As noted in Chapters One and Five, where parents' views of a child's ability are confirmed by a psychological assessment and the child is performing academically well below the level which would be expected, this indicates that the child has SEN, regardless of the actual level of his or her attainments. For example, a child who has been assessed as having intellectual ability within the average range whose reading, writing, spelling or number skills are well below average can be identified as having SEN, probably due to a specific learning difficulty. Likewise, a child who is recognised as being gifted, with well above average intellectual ability, whose attainments are at an average level, can also be identified as having SEN. However, both types of pupils may not be identified as having SEN by the school if its screening procedures do not include a suitable measure of cognitive ability and the child's teachers are not aware of the importance of being alert to possible discrepancies between intellectual ability and academic attainment.

It is therefore considered important for schools to have some means of assessing children's learning potential as a part of their identification procedures. This is not easy since measures of children's learning potential such as cognitive ability tests, and in particular IQ tests, are surrounded by controversy. However, it is an issue which schools cannot avoid. The best approach is considered to be the use of a combination of indicators of children's learning potential including the results of group tests of cognitive ability, clinical clues of their ability based on their teachers' observations, coupled with a willingness to take parents' views seriously. If there is some consensus among these indicators that there is a discrepancy between ability and attainment then an individual assessment by an educational psychologist should clarify the situation.

As well as reviewing their identification procedures schools should also review their assessment strategies for the pupils who have been identified as having SEN. Now that National Curriculum assessment data is becoming available this could provide useful information. There is also now a plethora of attainment and diagnostic tests which teachers can use to assess pupils identified as having SEN. It is up to SEN co-ordinators to make sure the school has a range of appropriate tests from which to select in assessing each child's SEN (see books on assessment of SEN and details of test publishers in the section following the References).

In addition to assessments conducted by school staff, in some cases more in-depth assessments will need to be carried out by outside specialists, such as those with expertise in assessing children with learning difficulties (educational psychologists) or sensory difficulties (teachers from hearing impaired and visually impaired services). In the future, assessments from some or all of these outside specialists will need to be bought in by the school. The challenge for SEN co-ordinators will then be to ensure that school-based assessment procedures are so effective that assessments by outside specialists will only be needed for a minority of children whose SEN are difficult to assess. However, given the expertise in assessment of SEN and the range of tests which it can be reasonably expected for schools to have, the importance of access to specialists' assessments from outside agencies cannot be underestimated.

Challenge 2: Establishing effective procedures for arranging provision and monitoring progress

Schools will be aiming to establish procedures similar to those described in Chapters Three and Four for implementing guidance from the Code on stages 1, 2 and 3 of the 5-stage model. A major part of this will be developing effective and efficient procedures for designing IEPs and reviews of progress. Although such procedures are well established in other parts of the world (such as the USA and New Zealand) they are new to most schools in the UK. Judging by the difficulties which have been experienced in other countries (for example, the USA) in setting up effective systems for designing and reviewing IEPs, there are likely to be considerable difficulties to overcome. Not the least of these will be staff resistance to changing their teaching strategies, coupled with their apprehension about working more closely with parents. SEN co-ordinators will need to make good use of the interpersonal skills discussed in Chapter Seven and the information on parental involvement discussed in Chapter Six to overcome these difficulties and address the challenge of establishing effective procedures for arranging provision and monitoring progress.

Challenge 3: Developing time-efficient procedures for collecting information and for keeping records

The necessity for collecting comprehensive information on children with SEN and on keeping detailed records is highlighted by the Code of Practice. There are three major reasons for the increased emphasis on record keeping. First, LEAs will be seeking evidence from schools regarding what has been done at stages 1 to 3 to inform their decisions at stages 4 and 5. Second, evidence of provisions implemented and progress made by pupils with SEN will be required for OFSTED inspections. Third, the school's records of action taken and contacts with parents will provide key evidence in the hopefully small number of cases which end up at the new SEN tribunals (see Rabinowicz and Friel, 1994) which are being set up to resolve disputes about provisions for individual children with SEN at stages 4 and 5.

The challenge for SEN co-ordinators is to be able to cope with the increased paper work without becoming so overwhelmed with administration that they have little time left for working with pupils with SEN. It is in recognition of the fact that SEN co-ordinators need to develop effective and efficient means of collecting and recording information that the proformas and checklists, such as those for conducting IEPs and reviews, have been provided in Chapters Three and Four and in the Appendices. It is also for this reason that sections on time management and stress management were included in Chapter Seven.

Challenge 4: *Developing effective consultation with parents and outside agencies*

The Code of Practice emphasises the importance for schools of liaising closely with parents of pupils with SEN and with outside agencies, including health and social services. These are areas in which many schools have had weaknesses in the past. With regard to outside agencies, there has generally been a difference between schools' relationships with LEA services and those provided by the health authority and social services. Schools have generally been much more comfortable about liaising with LEA staff than staff from either health or social services. Since the Code gives much more prominence to the involvement of health and social services in making provision for children with SEN, school staff, in particular SEN co-ordinators, will need to work hard to overcome existing barriers and develop effective channels for communication and consultation with these agencies.

With regard to working closely with parents, considerable emphasis is placed on this throughout the Code of Practice. Many schools already have effective procedures for liaising with parents but a large number of schools still operate in ways which tend to exclude parents. Given the increased parental rights embodied in recent education legislation and the increased expectations of their involvement in planning and reviewing the progress of their children with SEN required by the Code, schools can no longer afford *not* to work in partnership with parents.

Chapters Six and Seven of this handbook have been aimed at helping SEN co-ordinators and other teachers develop the competencies necessary for liaising effectively with parents and with personnel from agencies outside the school. The extent to which schools are able to meet this challenge will have considerable influence on the effectiveness of their overall provision for SEN.

Challenge 5: Ensuring accountability of funding and resources, both human and material

In the past there has been little accountability for the portion of the school's budget provided by the LEA for arranging provision for children with SEN (DES, 1992). With the implementation of the Code of Practice and the prospect of regular OFSTED inspections which will focus specifically on this issue (as noted in Chapter Eight) this situation is likely to change dramatically. From now on schools will need to identify specific spending on SEN from the school's budget. They will also need to justify the allocation of resources, financial, human and material, to different aspects of their provision for SEN. As the recent Audit Commission/HMI report (DES, 1992) pointed out, the key consideration regarding allocation of resources is what is achieved in terms of pupil gains.

In the past there has not only been a lack of awareness of how resources have been allocated but also a lack of evaluation of whether those resources were successful in achieving satisfactory pupil progress. The implementation of the 5-stage model for meeting SEN required by the Code of Practice will facilitate the evaluation of the adequacy of pupil progress. This will be accomplished by mechanisms such as reviews of children's IEPs and annual reviews of statements, which focus specifically on whether objectives which have been set have been attained or not. So, in the future, the information required for considering the accountability of SEN provision will be much more easily available.

The challenge for SEN co-ordinators will be to ensure optimum use of resources earmarked for SEN and to employ appropriate procedures for accounting for, and evaluating the effectiveness of, such things as the school's use of staff expertise in SEN. For example, is withdrawing pupils for small group tuition a more or less efficient use of staff resources than support teaching in the children's classrooms? In addition, what is the effectiveness of each strategy in facilitating children's progress? The lack of such evaluations, and therefore accountability, has been a major weakness of SEN provision in the past. It has led to some dubious guidance being provided to schools, for example, at least one LEA adviser on SEN attempted to dissuade schools from using resource rooms and withdrawal teaching, in favour of support teaching in ordinary classes, based on no evidence whatsoever of the effectiveness of these suggestions in terms of the progress of pupils with SEN.

Challenge 6: Establishing adequate pre-service and in-service training on the Code

In order that schools can effectively implement the principles and practices espoused by the Code, training needs to be provided for several groups within the field of education. The greatest priority is for SEN co-ordinators to receive guidance on the requirements of the Code and about developing procedures to meet these requirements within their own schools. It is intended that this handbook will contribute to this process and also provide SEN co-ordinators with materials for them to use in providing some in-service training for the next highest priority group, practising teachers. Other groups who will need training on the requirements of the Code are pre-service teachers and schools' SEN governors.

The challenge here is how to provide for these training needs with little or no money being provided by the Government for this purpose. As with other initiatives, there may be some GEST money available for a short period but this is unlikely to do much more than scrape the surface of the need for training brought about by the Code. This should be seen in the context of training for SEN generally which has experienced a major reduction in availability in recent years. For example, pre-service courses on SEN no longer exist and most of the 1-year full-time in-service diploma courses in SEN have closed down. Also, money is no longer widely available to support teachers doing advanced training in SEN at the master's degree level. In addition, now that at least 66 per cent of time on initial teacher training courses is spent in schools, mainly focusing on subject specialisms, there is little time for training these new teachers on various aspects of SEN, including the requirements of the Code.

CONCLUSION

The Code of Practice is likely to place considerable demands on teachers in mainstream schools in general and SEN co-ordinators in particular but it also has provided a great opportunity to substantially improve provisions for a large proportion of the children with SEN who attend mainstream schools. The extent to which this opportunity is taken up will be determined by how well the six challenges discussed in this chapter are met. It is intended that this handbook will help SEN co-ordinators to address these challenges and thereby contribute to the process of improvement in provisions for children with SEN which has been initiated by the publication of the Code of Practice.

References

Allan, J.A.B. and Nairne, J. (1984) *Class Discussions for Teachers and Counsellors in the Elementary School*. Toronto: University of Toronto Press.

Bastiani, J. (1989) *Working with Parents: A Whole School Approach*. Windsor: NFER-Nelson.

Black, R. (1987) *Getting Things Done*. London: Michael Joseph.

Bolton, R. (1979) *People Skills: How to Assert Yourself, Listen to Others and Resolve Conflicts*. Englewood Cliffs, NJ: Prentice-Hall.

Bower, S.A. and Bower, G.H. (1976) *Asserting Yourself*. Reading, MA: Addison-Wesley.

Brammer, L.M. (1993) *The Helping Relationship*, 5th edn. Englewood Cliffs, NJ: Prentice-Hall.

Broadfoot, P. (1989) *Reporting to Parents on Student Achievement: The UK Experience*. Working Paper 2/89, October, Bristol University.

Butt, N. and Scott, E.M. (1994) 'Individual education programmes in secondary schools', *Support for Learning*, 9 (1): 9–15.

Carpenter, B. and Stoneham, C. (1994) 'Inspection effectiveness: an analysis of an OFSTED inspection', *British Journal of Special Education*, 21 (2): 70–72.

Cautela, J.R. and Groden, J. (1978) *Relaxation*. Champaign, Ill.: Research Press.

Chorley, D. (1993) 'OFSTED prepares for special inspections', *British Journal of Special Education*, 20 (4): 127–128.

Cole, T. (1989) *Apart or a Part? Integration and the Growth of British Special Education*. Milton Keynes: Open University Press.

Covey, S.R. (1989) *Seven Habits of Highly Effective People*. New York: Simon & Schuster.

DES (1978) *The Warnock Report*. London: HMSO.

DES (1992) *Getting in on the Act. Provision for Pupils with Special Educational Needs: The National Picture (Audit Commission/HMI Report)*. London: HMSO.

DfE (1994) *Code of Practice on the Identification and Assessment of Special Educational Needs*. London: Department for Education.

DfE (1994) *The Organisation of Special Educational Provision (Circular 6/94)*. London: Department for Education.

Egan, G. (1982) *The Skilled Helper*, 2nd edn. Monterey, CA: Brooks/Cole.

Featherstone, H. (1981) *A Difference in the Family*. Harmondsworth: Penguin.

Ferner, J.D. (1980) *Successful Time Management*. New York: Wiley.

Fontana, D. (1993) *Managing Time*. Leicester: British Psychological Society.

Gawain, S. (1982) *Creative Visualization*. New York: Bantam.

Gordon, T. (1970) *Parent Effectiveness Training*. New York: Wyden.

Gross, J. (1993) *Special Educational Needs in the Primary School: A Practical Guide*. Buckingham: Open University Press.

Gulliford, R. and Upton, G. (eds) (1992) *Special Educational Needs*. London: Routledge.

Hall, E. and Hall, C. (1988) *Human Relations in Education*. London: Routledge.

Hallahan, D.P. and Kauffman, J.M. (1991) *Exceptional Children: Introduction to Special Education*, 5th edn. Boston, MA: Allyn & Bacon.

Harding, J. and Pike, G. (1988) *Parental Involvement in Secondary Schools*. London: ILEA Learning Resources Branch.

Hegarty, S. (1993) *Meeting Special Needs in Ordinary Schools: An Overview*, 2nd edn. London: Cassell.

Holland, S. and Ward, C. (1990) *Assertiveness: A Practical Approach*. Bicester: Winslow Press.

Hornby, G. (1989) 'A model for parent participation', *British Journal of Special Education*, 16 (4): 161–162.

Hornby, G. (1990) 'The organisation of parent involvement', *School Organisation*, 10 (2): 247–252.

Hornby, G. (1992) 'Integration of children with special educational needs: is it time for a policy review?', *Support for Learning*, 7 (3): 130–134.

Hornby, G. (1994) *Counselling in Child Disability: Skills for Working with Parents*. London: Chapman & Hall.

Hornby, G. (in press) *Working with Parents of Children with Special Needs*. London: Cassell.

Hornby, G. and Murray, R. (1983) 'Group programmes for parents of children with various handicaps', *Child: Care, Health and Development*, 9: 185–198.

Hughes, N. and Carpenter, B. (1991) 'Annual reviews: an active partnership', in R. Ashdown, B. Carpenter and K. Bovair (eds) *The Curriculum Challenge*. London: Falmer Press.

Hurt, J.S. (1988) *Outside the Mainstream: A History of Special Education*. London: Batsford.

Kroth, R.L. (1985) *Communicating with Parents of Exceptional Children*, 2nd edn. Denver: Love.

Landy, M. (1994) 'Preparation for school inspection', *Support for Learning*, 9 (1): 3–8.

Laurie, S.G. and Tucker, M.J. (1982) *Centering*. Wellingborough: Excalibur.

Leadbetter, J. and Leadbetter, P. (1993) *Special Children: Meeting the Challenge in the Primary School*. London: Cassell.

Lombana, J.H. (1983) *Home–School Partnerships: Guidelines and Strategies for Educators*. New York: Grune & Stratton.

Losoncy, L. (1982) *Think Your Way To Success*. Hollywood, CA: Wilshire.

Madders, J. (1979) *Stress and Relaxation*. Sydney: Collins.

Manthei, M. (1981) *Positively Me: A Guide to Assertive Behaviour*, revised edn. Auckland, NZ: Methuen.

Meichenbaum, D. (1985) *Stress Inoculation Training*. New York: Pergamon.

Mills, J.W. (1982) *Coping with Stress*. New York: Wiley.

OFSTED (1993) *Handbook for the Inspection of Schools*. London: HMSO.

Plowden, B. (Chair) (1967) *Children and Their Primary Schools*. London: HMSO.

Pugh, G. and De'Ath, E. (1984) *The Needs of Parents: Practice and Policy in Parent Education*. London: Macmillan.

Rabinowicz, J. and Friel, J. (1994) 'The new tribunal: first responses', *British Journal of Special Education*, 21 (1): 27–28.

Rogers, C.R. (1980) *A Way of Being*. Boston: Houghton Mifflin.

Scott, L. (1993) *Governors and Special Educational Needs*. London: Advisory Centre for Education.

Seligman, M. (1979) *Strategies for Helping Parents of Exceptional Children: A Guide for Teachers*. New York: Free Press.

Shaw, S.F., Bensky, J.M. and Dixon, B. (1981) *Stress and Burnout*. Reston, VA: Council for Exceptional Children.

Simpson, R.L. (1990) *Conferencing Parents of Exceptional Children*, 2nd edn. Austin, TX: PRO-ED.

Stakes, R. and Hornby, G. (1994) 'An evaluation of the changes in secondary school provisions for children with SEN in the years following the Warnock Report', paper submitted for publication.

Statham, J., MacKinnon, D. and Cathcart, H. (1989) *The Education Fact File*. London: Hodder & Stoughton.

Stone, L. (1993) 'Inspecting special: a new approach', *Special*, September, 33–37.

Swap, S.M. (1993) *Developing Home–School Partnerships*. New York: Teachers College Press.

Topping, K.J. (1986) *Parents as Educators: Training Parents to Teach Their Children*. London: Croom Helm.

Turla, P. and Hawkins, K.L. (1985) *Time Management Made Easy*. London: Grafton.

Turnbull, A.P. and Turnbull, H.R. (1986) *Families, Professionals and Exceptionality*. Columbus, OH: Merrill.

Wolfendale, S. (1988) *The Parental Contribution to Assessment*. Stratford-upon-Avon: National Council for Special Education.

Wolfendale, S. (1992) *Empowering Parents and Teachers*. London: Cassell.

Yalom, I.D. (1985) *The Theory and Practice of Group Psychotherapy*, 3rd edn. New York: Basic Books.

Useful Resources for SEN Co-ordinators

General Texts

Hegarty, S. (1993) *Meeting Special Needs in Ordinary Schools: An Overview*, 2nd edn. London: Cassell. Discusses a wide range of issues relevant to SEN provision in mainstream schools including the concept of SEN, integration, the 1981 and 1988 Education Acts, pupil grouping, staff training, parental involvement and support available from LEAs and special schools.

Male, J. and Thompson, C. (1985) *The Educational Implications of Disability: A Guide for Teachers*. London: Royal Association for Disability and Rehabilitation. Provides information on a wide range of disabilities and medical conditions and discusses the implications of these in terms of potential learning difficulties and classroom management.

Williams, P. (1991) *The Special Education Handbook: An Introductory Reference*. Milton Keynes: Open University Press. Provides information about over a thousand key terms and concepts encountered in the field of special education.

Primary Schools and SEN

Gross, J. (1993) *Special Educational Needs in the Primary School: A Practical Guide*. Buckingham: Open University Press. Covers a wide range of topics relevant to primary school teachers and SEN including: whole-school policy; SEN and the National Curriculum; assessment and record keeping; managing resources, behaviour and time; and SEN in reading, writing, maths and oral work.

Leadbetter, J. and Leadbetter, P. (1993) *Special Children: Meeting the Challenge in the Primary School*. London: Cassell. Provides comprehensive information related to SEN in primary schools including: the principles and practice of integration; approaches to teaching children with learning difficulties and behavioural difficulties; an overview of different types of SEN, recent legislation and early intervention programmes; and preparing pupils for transfer to secondary school.

Wolfendale, S. (1992) *Primary Schools and Special Needs: Policy, Planning and Provision*, 2nd edn. London: Cassell. Covers the major issues with regard to SEN provision in primary schools including: home–school relationships; management of behaviour and learning; organisation of curriculum, classroom and school; staff training; policy development; and secondary transfer.

Secondary Schools and SEN

Dean, J. (1989) *Special Needs in the Secondary School: The Whole School Approach*. London: Routledge. Provides a comprehensive overview of the organisation and management of SEN provision in secondary schools.

Sayer, J. (1994) *Secondary Schools for All? Strategies for Special Needs*, 2nd edn. London: Cassell. Discusses a wide range of issues related to provisions for pupils with SEN in secondary schools.

Stakes, R. (1995) *Teaching Children with Special Educational Needs in Secondary Schools*. Oxford: Nash Pollock. Provides practical information and ideas for teaching children with mild and moderate levels of SEN in secondary schools.

Children with Special Educational Needs: Overviews

Gillam, B. (ed.) (1986) *Handicapping Conditions in Children*. London: Croom Helm. Provides details about most of the major disabilities likely to be encountered in mainstream schools.

Gulliford, R. and Upton, G. (eds) (1992) *Special Educational Needs*. London: Routledge. Provides an overview of a wide range of types of special needs with 'state of the art' reviews on the education of each. Includes chapters on: learning difficulties; severe learning difficulties; speech and language difficulties; emotional and behavioural difficultues; visual impairments; hearing impairments; physical disabilities; psychological and health-related problems; multi-sensory impairments; curriculum issues; and management of special needs.

Hallahan, D.P. and Kauffman, J.M. (1991) *Exceptional Children: Introduction to Special Education*, 5th edn. Boston, MA: Allyn & Bacon. Provides a comprehensive overview of the major types of SEN, with chapters on mental handicap, specific learning difficulties, communication disorders, emotional/behavioural disorders, hearing impairment, visual impairment, physical disabilities and giftedness as well as separate chapters on parents/families and normalisation/integration.

Teaching Strategies for Children with SEN in Mainstream Schools

Lewis, R.B. and Doorlag, D.H. (1987) *Teaching Special Students in the Mainstream*, 2nd edn. Columbus, OH: Merrill. Covers teachers' skills and knowledge needed for effective mainstreaming of children with SEN. Includes chapters on: mild and specific learning difficulties; physical and health disabilities; communication problems; sensory difficulties; behavioural problems; and gifted pupils.

Stephens, T.M., Blackhurst, A.E. and Magliocca, L.A. (1988) *Teaching Main-streamed Students*, 2nd edn. Oxford: Pergamon. Focuses on effective techniques for educating children with SEN in mainstream schools. Includes chapters on obtaining and using assessment information, teaching social behaviour and study skills, the use of information technology, and working with parents.

Wade, B. and Moore, M. (1987) *Special Children ... Special Needs: Provision in Ordinary Classrooms*. London: Robert Royce. Discusses meeting SEN in ordinary schools with specific attention to children who are quiet, disruptive or have been abused. Other chapters consider difficulties with communication, reading and writing, whole-school policies and liaison. Individual chapters focus on children with hearing difficulties and those who are gifted.

Assessment

Salvia, J. and Ysseldyke, J.E. (1985) *Assessment in Special and Remedial Education*, 3rd edn. Boston, MA: Houghton Mifflin. Provides a comprehensive overview of issues regarding assessment of children with SEN and has detailed discussions of ability testing, attainment testing and diagnostic testing.

Wolfendale, S. (ed.) (1993) *Assessing Special Educational Needs*. London: Cassell. Contains chapters on a wide range of assessment issues related to SEN including: assessment for SEN in nursery education, primary schools, secondary schools and in further and higher education; and parental involvement in assessment.

Parental Involvement

Hornby, G. (1994) *Counselling in Child Disability: Skills for Working with Parents*. London: Chapman & Hall. Discusses the effects of childhood disability on parents and elaborates on the interpersonal skills needed by teachers in order to work effectively with parents and outside specialists.

Hornby, G. (in press) *Working with Parents of Children with Special Needs*. London: Cassell. Discusses a wide range of strategies which teachers can use to establish effective working relationships with parents and enhance the development of their children with SEN.

Wolfendale, S. (1988) *The Parental Contribution to Assessment*. Stratford-upon-Avon: National Council for Special Education. Discusses issues and strategies to do with improving parental involvement in the assessment process.

Consultation/Interpersonal Skills

Bolton, R. (1979) *People Skills: How to Assert Yourself, Listen to Others and Resolve Conflicts*. Englewood Cliffs, NJ: Prentice-Hall. Covers the communication and interpersonal skills needed by teachers in their liaison role, including listening, conflict resolution and problem solving.

Jordan, A. (1994) *Skills in Collaborative Classroom Consultation*. London: Routledge. Provides a model of consultation for teachers of children with SEN which involves contracting, assessment, feedback and developing plans of action. Specific chapters discuss difficult consulting situations and working with parents and outside specialists.

Management

Jones, N. and Southgate, T. (eds) (1989) *The Management of Special Needs in Ordinary Schools*. London: Routledge. Contains chapters on a wide range of management issues regarding SEN in mainstream schools including: school policies; pastoral care; integration; teaching strategies; open learning; gifted pupils; in-service training; and information technology.

Walters, B. (1994) *Management for Special Needs*. London: Cassell. Provides an overview of management issues including mission statements, policy development, LMS, quality assurance and marketing.

Mild and Moderate Learning Difficulties

Dockrell, J. and McShane, J. (1992) *Children's Learning Difficulties: A Cognitive Approach*. Includes chapters on assessment and intervention with mild, moderate and severe learning difficulties. Has separate chapters on reading, number and language difficulties.

Montgomery, D. (1990) *Children with Learning Difficulties*. London: Cassell. Discusses the theory and practice of curriculum development, behaviour management and pedagogy with children with learning difficulties.

Westwood, P. (1993) *Commonsense Methods for Children with Special Needs*, 2nd edn. London: Routledge. This is an excellent source of practical guidance for teaching children with learning difficulties in mainstream schools. It includes chapters on the development of reading, writing and numeracy skills, adapting the curriculum, social skills, behaviour management and teaching strategies.

Severe, Profound and Multiple Learning Difficulties

Coupe, J. and Porter, J. (eds) (1986) *The Education of Children with Severe Learning Difficulties*. Beckenham: Croom Helm. Contains chapters on most aspects of education of children with SLD.

Tilstone, T. (ed.) (1991) *Teaching Pupils with Severe Learning Difficulties: Practical Approaches*. London: David Fulton. Covers a wide range of aspects relevant to teaching children with SLD.

Specific Learning Difficulties

Miles, T.R. and Miles, E. (1990) *Dyslexia: A Hundred Years On*. Milton Keynes: Open University Press. Provides an overview of the field, the history, current research and teaching methods and programmes.

Pumfrey, P. and Reason, R. (1991) *Specific Learning Difficulties (Dyslexia): Challenges and Responses*. Windsor: NFER-NELSON. Provides a summary of current knowledge on the educational, psychological and medical aspects of specific learning difficulties.

Emotional and Behavioural Difficulties

Charlton, T. and David, K. (eds) (1993) *Managing Misbehaviour in Schools*, 2nd edn. London: Routledge. Takes a broad view of the management of behavioural problems. Includes chapters on counselling and behavioural approaches, pastoral care, working with parents and liaison with other agencies.

Cooper, P., Smith, C.J. and Upton, G. (1994) *Emotional and Behavioural Difficulties: Theory into Practice*. London: Routledge. Covers a wide range of approaches for working with pupils with EBD including counselling, behavioural management and family therapy, as well as considering other factors such as school policies and overall school effectiveness.

Smith, C.J. and Laslett, R. (1993) *Effective Classroom Management: A Teacher's Guide*. London: Routledge. Provides practical advice for classroom teachers on dealing with disruptive pupils.

Physical Disabilities

Bleck, E.E. and Nagle, D.A. (1975) *Physically Handicapped Children: A Medical Atlas for Teachers*. New York: Grune & Stratton. Contains detailed and well-illustrated information about all physical disabilities likely to be encountered in schools.

Halliday, P. (1989) *Children with Physical Disabilities*. London: Cassell. Discusses different aspects of physical disability including curricular and extra-curricular implications and its management in the school setting.

Hearing Difficulties

Reed, M. (1984) *Educating Hearing Impaired Children: In Ordinary and Special Schools*. Milton Keynes: Open University Press. Provides a comprehensive overview of issues and information relevant to teachers of children with hearing difficulties. Includes chapters on: nature of hearing impairment; emotional and social consequences; medical aspects; identification and assessment; communication; hearing aids; educational services; parents as educators; and additional disabilities.

Webster, A. and Wood, D. (1989) *Children with Hearing Difficulties*. London:

Cassell. This book is aimed at teachers of children with hearing difficulties in ordinary schools and includes chapters on hearing loss, deafness and the learning process, and teaching strategies.

Visual Difficulties

Best, A.B. (1992) *Teaching Children with Visual Impairments*. Milton Keynes: Open University Press. A comprehensive overview for teachers of children with visual difficulties in primary, secondary or special schools which contains many practical examples and illustrations. Chapters focus on a wide range of topics including educational services, access to the curriculum teaching methods, tactile skills, use of residual vision, listening skills and mobility.

Chapman, E.K. and Stone, J.M. (1988) *The Visually Handicapped Child in Your Classroom*. London: Cassell. Provides discussion of issues and information relevant to teaching children with visual difficulties in mainstream schools. Includes chapters on educational issues, management of the environment, curriculum access and adaptation, and the use of technological aids.

Speech and Language Difficulties

Syder, D. (1992) *An Introduction to Communication Disorders*. London: Chapman & Hall. Provides a description of the major speech and language difficulties including articulation problems, delayed language, stammering and voice disorders along with suggestions for intervention.

A chapter on 'communication disorders' in Hallahan and Kauffman (1991, cited above) provides an overview of the various speech and language difficulties encountered in mainstream schools along with brief details of the intervention strategies used to deal with them.

Medical Conditions

Batshaw, M.L., Perret, Y.M. and Carter, W.P. (1992) *Children with Disabilities: A Medical Primer*, 3rd edn. Baltimore: Paul H. Brookes. Contains detailed medical information on a wide range of disabilities.

Lansdown, R. (1980) *More than Sympathy: The Everyday Needs of Sick and Handicapped Children and their Families*. London: Tavistock. Provides brief details of the medical conditions most likely to be encountered in mainstream schools, including diabetes, epilepsy, asthma, cystic fibrosis, muscular dystrophy, heart disease, leukaemia and spina bifida.

Gifted

Borland, J.H. (1989) *Planning and Implementing Programs for the Gifted*. New York: Teachers College Press. Discusses identification, assessment and curriculum planning for gifted children.

Milgram, R.M. (ed.) (1991) *Counselling Gifted and Talented Children: A Guide for Teachers, Counselors and Parents*. Norwood, NJ: Ablex. A useful compendium of ideas for working with gifted pupils and their parents. Includes chapters on: identification; special education options; differentiating instruction; and gifted children with specific learning difficulties.

Test Publishers

Hodder & Stoughton, 338 Euston Road, London, NW1 3BH. Tel.: 071 873 6000.

LDA, Duke Street, Wisbech, Cambs, PE13 2AE. Tel.: 0945 63441.

Macmillan, Houndmills, Basingstoke, Hampshire, RG21 2XS. Tel.: 0256 29242.

NFER-NELSON, Darville House, 2 Oxford Road East, Windsor, Berkshire, SL4 1DF. Tel.: 0753 858961.

Psychological Corporation, Foots Cray High Street, Sidcup, Kent, DA14 5HP. Tel.: 081 300 3322.

Appendices

The materials in these appendices may be

reproduced free-of-charge for use in your school.

TO _____
      (CLASS TEACHER/FORM TUTOR/YEAR TUTOR)

NAME OF PUPIL _____ FORM _____

REASON FOR CONCERN (Please give evidence, including test results, NC levels etc., where available.)

SIGNED _____ DATE _____/_____/_____

A1 Sample proforma for expression of concern   © Routledge

PRESENT _____

DATE _____/_____/_____

SUMMARY OF DISCUSSION

DECISIONS TAKEN

DATE OF REVIEW

SIGNED _____
        (CLASS TEACHER/FORM TUTOR/YEAR TUTOR)

A2 Sample proforma for record of initial meeting   © Routledge

NAME _____ FORM _____

DATE OF BIRTH _____/_____/_____

DATE	ACTION TAKEN

	INFORMATION (where appropriate)	
	REQUESTED (date)	RECEIVED (date)
1 SCHOOL		
CLASS RECORDS (a) Current (b) Past (c) From previous school		
NC ATTAINMENTS		
TEST RESULTS		
RECORDS OF ACHIEVEMENT		
OTHER SOURCES (a) About education (b) About behaviour		
KNOWN HEALTH PROBLEMS		
KNOWN SOCIAL PROBLEMS		
2 PARENTS		
GENERAL DEVELOPMENT		
GENERAL HEALTH		
PERCEPTION OF (a) Performance (i) At home (ii) At school (b) Behaviour (i) At home (ii) At school (c) Progress (i) At home (ii) At school		
ADDITIONAL FACTORS		
OTHER AGENCIES OR INDIVIDUALS TO BE INVOLVED		
3 CHILD		
PERCEPTION OF DIFFICULTIES		
HOW THESE DIFFICULTIES SHOULD BE ADDRESSED		
OTHERS TO BE INVOLVED		
4 FURTHER INFORMATION, WITH THE AGREEMENT OF PARENTS, TO BE GATHERED FROM		
SCHOOL DOCTOR		
FAMILY DOCTOR		
SOCIAL SERVICES		
EDUCATION WELFARE OFFICER		
LOCAL EDUCATION AUTHORITY		
ANY OTHER AGENCIES (please specify)		

A4 Information checklist © Routledge

_____ SCHOOL

ADDITIONAL HELP AT STAGE 1

SECTION 1
NAME: _____ FORM: _____ DATE OF BIRTH: ____/____/_____
DATE OF PLAN: __/__/__ REVIEW DATE: __/__/__
CIRCULATION: PARENTS, HEAD, SEN CO-ORDINATOR, OTHERS _____
PEOPLE TO BE INVOLVED IN THE REVIEW: PARENTS, SEN CO-ORDINATOR,
OTHERS _____

SECTION 2
REASONS FOR IDENTIFICATION: _____

SECTION 3
ACTION TO BE TAKEN: _____

TARGETS: _____

MONITORING ARRANGEMENTS: _____

SECTION 4
REVIEW (including progress made with evidence where appropriate): _____

RECOMMENDATIONS FOR FUTURE ACTION: _____

SIGNED: _____ DATE: __/__/__

PLEASE COMPLETE THE REVIEW SECTION ABOVE WHEN APPROPRIATE AND RETURN
THIS FORM TO _____ BY __/__/__

A5 Sample proforma for giving help at stage 1   © Routledge

_____ SCHOOL

REVIEW OF HELP GIVEN AT STAGE 1
REVIEW NO. _____

NAME: _____ FORM: _____ DATE OF BIRTH: __/__/__

DATE OF REVIEW: __/__/__

PRESENT: _____

1. SUMMARY OF PROGRESS MADE: _____
_____
_____
_____
_____
_____

2. VIEWS OF PARENT: _____
_____
_____

3. VIEWS OF CHILD: _____
_____
_____

4. EFFECTIVENESS OF PLAN: _____
_____
_____
_____

5. UPDATED/ADDITIONAL INFORMATION: _____
_____
_____

6. FUTURE ACTION: (please tick as appropriate)

(a) No further action ☐

(b) Continue at stage 1 ☐

(c) Move to stage 2 ☐

RECOMMENDATIONS FOR IEP AT STAGE 2: (if appropriate) _____
_____
_____
_____
_____
_____

SIGNED: _____ (parent)

_____ (child if appropriate)

_____ (class/year teacher)

A6 Sample proforma for use at a review at stage 1   © Routledge

_____ SCHOOL

INDIVIDUAL EDUCATION PLAN
STAGE 2

SECTION 1

NAME: _____ FORM: _____ DATE OF BIRTH: ____/____/___

DATE OF PLAN: __/__/__ REVIEW DATE: __/__/__

CIRCULATION*: PARENTS, HEAD, CLASS TEACHER, OTHERS

_____

PEOPLE TO BE INVOLVED IN THE REVIEW: PARENTS, SEN CO-ORDINATOR, OTHERS _____

SECTION 2

REASONS FOR IDENTIFICATION: _____

_____

_____

_____

_____

_____

_____

_____

SECTION 3

REVIEW (including progress made with evidence where appropriate): _____

_____

_____

_____

_____

_____

RECOMMENDATIONS FOR FUTURE ACTION: _____

_____

_____

_____

_____

SIGNED: _____ DATE: __/__/__

PLEASE COMPLETE THE REVIEW SECTION ABOVE WHEN APPROPRIATE AND RETURN THIS FORM TO _____ (SENCO) BY __/__/__

A7 Sample proforma for an IEP at stage 2 in a primary school   © Routledge

SECTION 4

1. CURRICULAR NEEDS

(a) Priorities: _____
_____
_____

(b) Learning objectives: _____
_____
_____

(c) Criteria for success: _____
_____
_____

(d) Monitoring and review
     arrangements: _____
_____
_____

2. TEACHING ARRANGEMENTS

(a) Strategies and techniques: _____
_____
_____

(b) Equipment and materials: _____
_____
_____

3. NON-CURRICULAR NEEDS

(a) Pastoral care arrangements: _____
_____
_____

(b) Medical requirements: _____
_____
_____
_____

SECTION 5

STAFF ACTION PLAN*

(a) _____
_____
_____

(b) _____
_____
_____

(c) _____
_____
_____

(d) _____
_____
_____

(a) _____
_____
_____

(b) _____
_____
_____

(a) _____
_____
_____

(b) _____
_____
_____

Notes

NB. Section 4 is to be completed by the SEN co-ordinator before being circulated.

*Staff identified in section 1 who have a teaching role with the pupil should complete section 5 on receipt of this plan.

_____ SCHOOL

INDIVIDUAL EDUCATION PLAN
STAGE 2

SECTION 1

NAME: _____ FORM: _____ DATE OF BIRTH: ___/___/___

DATE OF PLAN: ___/___/___ REVIEW DATE: ___/___/___

CIRCULATION*: PARENTS, HEAD, SEN CO-ORDINATOR, HEAD OF YEAR,
FORM TUTOR, SUBJECT STAFF

_____

PEOPLE TO BE INVOLVED IN THE REVIEW: PARENTS, SEN CO-ORDINATOR,
OTHERS _____

SECTION 2

REASONS FOR IDENTIFICATION: _____
_____
_____
_____
_____
_____
_____
_____

SECTION 3

REVIEW (including progress made with evidence where appropriate): _____
_____
_____
_____
_____
_____

RECOMMENDATIONS FOR FUTURE ACTION: _____
_____
_____
_____

SIGNED: _____ DATE: ___/___/___

PLEASE COMPLETE THE REVIEW SECTION ABOVE WHEN APPROPRIATE AND
RETURN THIS FORM TO _____ (SENCO) BY ___/___/___

A8 Sample proforma for an IEP at stage 2 in a secondary school © Routledge

SECTION 4

1. CURRICULAR NEEDS

    (a)   Priorities: _____

_____

_____

_____

    (b)   Learning objectives: _____

_____

_____

_____

    (c)   Criteria for success: _____

_____

_____

_____

    (d)   Monitoring and review
          arrangements: _____

_____

_____

2. TEACHING ARRANGEMENTS

    (a)   Strategies and techniques: _____

_____

_____

_____

    (b)   Equipment and materials: _____

_____

_____

3. NON-CURRICULAR NEEDS

    (a)   Pastoral care arrangements: _____

_____

_____

_____

    (b)   Medical requirements: _____

_____

_____

_____

SECTION 5

STAFF ACTION PLAN*

    (a) _____

_____

_____

_____

    (b) _____

_____

_____

_____

    (c) _____

_____

_____

_____

    (d) _____

_____

_____

    (a) _____

_____

_____

_____

    (b) _____

_____

_____

    (a) _____

_____

_____

_____

    (b) _____

_____

_____

_____

Notes

NB. Section 4 is to be completed by the SEN co-ordinator before being circulated.

*Staff identified in section 1 who have a teaching role with the pupil should complete section
 5 on receipt of this plan.

_____ SCHOOL

REVIEW OF INDIVIDUAL EDUCATION PLAN
STAGE 2: REVIEW NO. _____

NAME: _____ FORM: _____ DATE OF BIRTH: ___/___/_____

DATE OF REVIEW: __/__/__

PRESENT: _____

1. SUMMARY OF PROGRESS MADE: _____
_____
_____
_____
_____
_____
_____

2. VIEWS OF PARENT: _____
_____
_____

3. VIEWS OF CHILD: _____
_____
_____

4. EFFECTIVENESS OF PLAN: _____
_____
_____
_____

5. UPDATED/ADDITIONAL INFORMATION: _____
_____
_____

6. FUTURE ACTION: (please tick as appropriate)

   (a) REVERT TO STAGE 1
   (b) NEW IEP AT STAGE 2
   (c) MOVE TO STAGE 3

SUPPORT SERVICE(S) TO BE INVOLVED AT STAGE 3 _____
_____

RECOMMENDATIONS FOR NEW IEP: (if appropriate) _____
_____
_____
_____
_____
_____

SIGNED: _____ (parent)
         _____ (child if appropriate)
         _____ (SEN co-ordinator)

A9 Sample proforma for use at a review at stage 2   © Routledge

Does your school have:

- a whole-school policy for record keeping?
- effective means of collecting information – from previous or feeder schools, other services and agencies etc.?
- a range of effective screening procedures?
- an SEN link teacher in each subject department? (secondary schools)
- a whole-school policy for reporting to parents?
- a whole-school policy for identifying and recording progress?
- a suitable, private room for consultation with parents?
- a policy for INSET on SEN for non-specialist staff?
- INSET provision on SEN?

For an individual child has the class/year teacher:

- clearly specified the cause for concern?
- collected the appropriate information?
- collected reports on the child in the school setting from appropriate sources?
- informed the head teacher, the SEN co-ordinator and those with parental responsibility that the child is being considered under stage 1 procedures?
- discussed the situation with those with parental responsibility and sought their views?
- contacted any other agencies or individuals whom those with parental responsibility would like involved?
- sought the views of the child?
- collected information from the child's GP and/or social services and/or educational welfare service as agreed with those with parental responsibility, if appropriate?

Does the INDIVIDUAL EDUCATION PLAN set out:

- the nature of the learning difficulties experienced?
- learning objectives and targets to be achieved?
- the timespan in which to achieve targets?
- the staff to be involved?
- the frequency of any support to be given?
- any specific programmes and/or activities to be used?
- any parental help to be given?
- criteria for success?
- monitoring and recording arrangements?
- the teaching strategies and techniques to be used?
- the equipment and materials to be used?
- any pastoral care arrangements?
- any medical requirements?
- the review date?
- the people to be involved with the review?

A10 Checklist on stages 1 and 2 policy and practice

_____ SCHOOL

INDIVIDUAL EDUCATION PLAN

STAGE 3

SECTION 1

NAME: _____ FORM: _____ DATE OF BIRTH: ____/____/_____

DATE OF PLAN: __/__/__ REVIEW DATE: __/__/__

SUPPORT SERVICE(S) INVOLVED _____

CONTACT PERSON(S) _____ TEL. _____

_____ TEL. _____

CIRCULATION*: PARENTS, SUPPORT SERVICE(S), HEAD, CLASS TEACHER, OTHERS

_____

PEOPLE TO BE INVOLVED IN THE REVIEW: PARENTS, SEN CO-ORDINATOR, SUPPORT

SERVICE CONTACT(S), CLASS TEACHER, OTHERS

_____

SECTION 2
REASONS FOR IDENTIFICATION: _____
_____
_____
_____
_____
_____

SECTION 3
REVIEW (including progress made with evidence where appropriate):
   (a) School _____
   _____
   _____
   _____
   _____

   (b) Support service _____
   _____
   _____
   _____
   _____

RECOMMENDATIONS FOR FUTURE ACTION:
   (a) School _____
   _____
   _____
   _____
   _____

   (b) Support service _____
   _____
   _____
   _____
   _____
   _____

SIGNED: _____ DATE: __/__/__

PLEASE RETURN TO _____ (SENCO) BY __/__/__

A11 Sample proforma for an IEP at stage 3 in a primary school   © Routledge

SECTION 4	SECTION 5
1. CURRICULAR NEEDS	STAFF ACTION PLAN*
(a) Priorities: _____	(a) _____
(b) Learning objectives: _____	(b) _____
(c) Criteria for success: _____	(c) _____
(d) Monitoring and review arrangements: _____	(d) _____
2. TEACHING ARRANGEMENTS	
(a) Strategies and techniques: _____	(a) _____
(b) Equipment and materials: _____	(b) _____
3. NON-CURRICULAR NEEDS	
(a) Pastoral care arrangements: ___	(a) _____
(b) Medical requirements: _____	(b) _____

Notes

NB. Section 4 is to be completed by the SEN co-ordinator before this plan is circulated.

*Staff identified in section 1 who have a teaching role with the pupil should complete section 5 on receipt of this plan.

_____ SCHOOL

INDIVIDUAL EDUCATION PLAN
STAGE 3

SECTION 1

NAME: _____ FORM: _____ DATE OF BIRTH: _____/_____/_____

DATE OF PLAN: __/__/__ REVIEW DATE: __/__/__

SUPPORT SERVICE(S) INVOLVED _____

CONTACT PERSON(S) _____ TEL. _____

_____ TEL. _____

CIRCULATION*: PARENTS, SUPPORT SERVICE(S), HEAD, SEN CO-ORDINATOR, HEAD OF YEAR, FORM TUTOR, SUBJECT STAFF

_____

PEOPLE TO BE INVOLVED IN THE REVIEW: PARENTS, SEN CO-ORDINATOR, SUPPORT SERVICE CONTACT(S), OTHERS

_____

SECTION 2
REASONS FOR IDENTIFICATION: _____
_____
_____
_____
_____
_____

SECTION 3
REVIEW (including progress made with evidence where appropriate):
  (a) School _____
_____
_____
_____
_____

  (b) Support service _____
_____
_____
_____
_____

RECOMMENDATIONS FOR FUTURE ACTION:
  (a) School _____
_____
_____
_____

  (b) Support service _____
_____
_____
_____
_____

SIGNED: _____ DATE: __/__/__

PLEASE RETURN TO _____ (SENCO) BY __/__/__

A12 Sample proforma for an IEP at stage 3 in a secondary school © Routledge

SECTION 4	SECTION 5
1. CURRICULAR NEEDS	**STAFF ACTION PLAN***
(a) Priorities: _____	(a) _____
(b) Learning objectives: _____	(b) _____
(c) Criteria for success: _____	(c) _____
(d) Monitoring and review arrangements: _____	(d) _____
2. TEACHING ARRANGEMENTS	
(a) Strategies and techniques: ____	(a) _____
(b) Equipment and materials: ____	(b) _____
3. NON-CURRICULAR NEEDS	
(a) Pastoral care arrangements: ___	(a) _____
(b) Medical requirements: _____	(b) _____

Notes

NB. Section 4 is to be completed by the SEN co-ordinator before this plan is circulated.

*Staff identified in section 1 who have a teaching role with the pupil should complete section 5 on receipt of this plan.

_____ SCHOOL

REVIEW OF INDIVIDUAL EDUCATION PLAN
STAGE 3: REVIEW NO. _____

SECTION 1
NAME: _____ FORM: _____ DATE OF BIRTH: ____/____/_____
DATE OF REVIEW: __/__/__
PRESENT: _____

SECTION 2
1. SUMMARY OF PROGRESS MADE:
    (a) School: _____
    _____
    _____
    _____

    (b) Support service: _____
    _____
    _____
    _____
    _____

2. VIEWS OF PARENT: _____
    _____
    _____
    _____

3. VIEWS OF CHILD: _____
    _____

4. EFFECTIVENESS OF PLAN: _____
    _____
    _____
    _____
    _____
    _____
    _____

5. UPDATED/ADDITIONAL INFORMATION: _____
    _____
    _____
    _____

SECTION 3
6. FUTURE ACTION: (please tick as appropriate)

    (a)   Revert to stage 2   ☐
    (b)   New IEP at stage 2   ☐   Stage 3   ☐
    (c)(i) Support service(s) to be involved: _____
    _____

(d)   Move to stage 4   ☐

RECOMMENDATIONS FOR NEW IEP: _____
_____
_____
_____
_____
_____

SIGNED: _____ (parent)
        _____ (child if appropriate)
        _____ (support service)
        _____ (support service)
        _____ (SEN co-ordinator)

A13 Sample proforma for use at a review at stage 3   © Routledge

Organisation and address	Contact person	Tel. no.

School contacts

Organisation and address   Contact person   Tel. no.

- LEA special needs officer
- SEN section

LEA support services

- SEN adviser
- School adviser
- Educational psychologist
- Learning support
- Behaviour support
- Physical handicap
- Hearing impairment
- Visual impairment
- Travellers' children
- Bi-lingual
- Education welfare
- Advisory teachers
- Portage service
- Hospital tuition
- Home tuition
- IT support

Other agencies

- Health authority
- Speech therapy
- Community health
- School nurse
- Adolescent psychiatric service
- Social services
- Neighbourhood team

Other schools

- Local pyramid SEN co-ordinators
- Local special schools

Local parent support groups

Any other contacts

A14 Checklist of specialists, agencies and organisations   © Routledge

NAME _____ FORM _____

DATE OF BIRTH_____ DATE OF STATEMENT _____

(a) Main aspects of pupil's needs

(b) Provision stated

(c) How being met?

1

2

3

4

5

6

EXPECTED REVIEW DATE _____

A15 Summary and monitoring form for pupils with statements © Routledge

This form is intended to help parents optimise their involvement in the assessment process by providing comprehensive information on the child in the home setting. Please comment on the following aspects of your child's development and add any further information which you consider important.

- *Health*: e.g. medical problems, medication taken, eating and sleeping habits

- *Physical*: e.g. walking, climbing, jumping, throwing

- *Eye–hand co-ordination*: e.g. stacking blocks, threading, drawing shapes, assembling objects

- *Self-help*: e.g. dressing, grooming, handling money, travelling independently

- *Communication*: e.g. clarity of speech, vocabulary, length of sentences, fluency

- *Basic academic skills*: e.g. reading, writing, spelling, number skills

- *Work habits*: e.g. concentration span, study skills, memory

- *Play/leisure*: e.g. reading, hobbies, sporting activities, club membership

- *Behaviour*: e.g. overactive, nervous, defiant, moody

- *Relationships*: e.g. with siblings, friends, adults

- *Any other comments*:

A16 Sample parent assessment form   © Routledge

This form is intended to help parents optimise their involvement in the review process by providing comprehensive information on the child in the home setting. Please complete the following sections with any changes which have occurred since the previous review. Then add any further information which you consider important.

- *General health*: e.g. illnesses, fitness

- *General behaviour*: e.g. is less disobedient at home

- *Abilities*: e.g. progress in dressing self and in grooming

- *Likes and dislikes*: e.g. has shown less interest in reading

- *Independence*: e.g. can now catch a bus by herself

- *Priority areas*: e.g. weaknesses to overcome, strengths to develop

- *Home circumstances*: e.g. addition to the family, death of family member

- *Any other comments*:

- statement of guiding principle of partnership between parents and teachers;

- statement of open-door policy regarding parents;

- procedures for establishing two-way communication between home and school;

- arrangements for recording and acting on concerns raised by parents;

- procedures for involving parents when a concern is first raised within the school;

- arrangements for optimising parent involvement in assessments and reviews of progress;

- procedures for ensuring that parents are kept informed about school organisation;

- procedures for reporting to parents on their children's progress;

- availability of parent education, guidance and support;

- opportunities for parents to reinforce school programmes at home;

- opportunities for parents who wish to do voluntary work at the school;

- opportunities for parents to become involved in the work of PTA or Governors;

- availability of a parents' room.

A18 Checklist of elements to include in school policy for parental involvement

A19 USEFUL ADDRESSES

Organisation and address	*Local contact*	*Tel. no.*

Advisory Centre for Education
18 Aberdeen Studios
22 Highbury Grove
London NW1 2SD
071 833 2041

AFASIC
347 Central Market
Smithfield
London EC1A 9NH
071 236 3632

Association for Brain
　Damaged Children
47 Northumberland Road
Coventry CV1 3AP
0203 25617

Association for Spina Bifida and
　Hydrocephalus
Ashbah House
42 Park Road
Peterborough PE1 2UQ
0733 555988

British Diabetic Association
10 Queen Anne Street
London W1M 0BD
071 323 1521

British Dyslexia Association
98 London Road
Reading RG1 5AU
0734 668271

British Epilepsy Association
Anstey House
40 Hanover Square
Leeds LS3 1BE
0531 439393

Organisation and address	Local contact	Tel. no.

British Sports Association for the
 Disabled
Hayward House
Barnard Crescent
Aylesbury
Bucks HP21 0PG
0296 27889

Brittle Bone Society
Ward 8
Strathmartine Hospital
Strathmartine
Dundee DD3 0PG
0382 817771

Centre for Studies on Integration in
 Education
4th Floor
415 Edgware Road
London NW2 6NB
081 452 8642

The Children's Society
Edward Rudolph House
Margery Street
London WC1X 0JL
071 837 4299

Contact-a-Family
170 Tottenham Court Road
London W1P 0HA
071 383 3555

Council for Disabled Children
c/o National Children's Bureau
8 Wakley Street
London EC1V 7QE
071 278 9441

Cystic Fibrosis Research Trust
Alexandra House
5 Blyth Road
Bromley
Kent BR1 3RS
081 464 7211

Organisation and address	*Local contact*	*Tel. no.*

Disabled Living Foundation
380–384 Harrow Road
London W9 2HU
071 289 6111

Down's Syndrome Association
155 Mitcham Road
London SW17 9PG
081 682 4001

Dyslexia Institute
133 Gresham Road
Staines
Middlesex TW18 2AJ
0784 463851

Family Fund
Joseph Rowntree Memorial Trust
PO Box 50
York YO1 1UY
0904 621115

Friedrich's Ataxia Group
The Common
Cranleigh
Surrey GU8 8SB
0483 27274

Haemophilia Society
123 Westminster Bridge Road
London SE1 7HR
071 928 2020

Handicapped Adventure Playground
    Association
Fulham Palace
Bishops Avenue
London SW6 6EA
071 736 4443

Huntington's Disease Association
108 Battersea High Street
London SW11 3HP
071 223 7000

Organisation and address	*Local contact*	*Tel. no.*

Hyperactive Children's Support Group
71 Whyke Lane
Chichester
Sussex PO19 2LD
0903 725182

Independent Panel for Special Education
  Advice
84 Seymour Park Road
Marlow
Bucks SL7 3EW
0628 478986

In Touch
10 Norman Road
Sale
Cheshire M33 3DF
061 962 4441

Kids
80 Wayneflete Square
London W10 6UD
081 969 2817

Leukaemia Care Society
PO Box 82
Exeter
Devon EX2 5DP
0392 218514

MENCAP
117–123 Golden Lane
London EC1Y 0RT
071 454 0454

MIND
22 Harley Street
London W1N 2ED
071 637 0741

Motability
Gate House
Westgate
The High
Harlow
Essex CM10 1HR
0279 635666

Organisation and address	*Local contact*	*Tel. no.*

Muscular Dystrophy Group of GB
7–11 Prescott Place
London SW4 6BS
071 720 8055

National Association for the Education of
    Sick Children
Open School
18 Victoria Park Square
London E2 9PF
081 980 6263

National Association for Gifted Children
Park Campus
Boughton Green Road
Northampton NN2 7AL
0604 792300

National Association of Governors and
    Managers (NAGM)
Suite 36/38
21 Bennetts Hill
Birmingham B2 5QP
021 643 5787

National Association for Special
    Educational Needs (NASEN)
York House
Exhall Grange
Wheelwright Lane
Coventry CV7 9HP
0203 362414

National Autistic Society
276 Willesden Lane
London NW2 5RB
081 451 1114

National Children's Bureau
8 Wakley Street
London EC1V 7QE
071 278 9441

National Deaf Children's Society
45 Hereford Road
London W2 5AH
071 229 9272

Organisation and address	*Local contact*	*Tel. no.*

National Eczema Society
4 Tavistock Place
London WC1H 9RA
071 388 4097

National Federation of the Blind
of the UK
Unity House
Smyth Street
Westgate
Wakefield WF1 1ER
0924 291313

National Library for the Handicapped
Child
Ash Court
Rose Street
Wokingham
Berks RG11 1XS
0734 89110

National Physically Handicapped and
Able Bodied (PHAB)
Padholme Road East
Peterborough PE1 5UL
0733 54117

National Toy Libraries Association
68 Churchway
London NW1 1LT
071 387 9592

Network 81
1–7 Woodfield Terrace
Chapel Hill
Stansted
Essex CM24 8AJ
0279 647415

Neuro-Fibromatosis Association
120 London Road
Kingston upon Thames
KT2 6QJ
081 547 1636

Organisation and address	*Local contact*	*Tel. no.*

Parents in Partnership
Unit 2
Ground Floor
70 South Lambert Road
London SW8 1RL
071 735 7733

Pre-school Playgroup Association
61–63 Kings Cross Road
London WC1X 9LL
071 833 0991

Royal Association for Disability and
   Rehabilitation (RADAR)
12 City Forum
250 City Road
London EC1V 8AF
071 250 3222

Royal National Institute for the Blind
224 Great Portland Street
London W1N 6AA
071 388 1266

Royal National Institute for the Deaf
105 Gower Street
London WC1E 6AH
071 387 8033

Sense
11–13 Clifton Terrace
Finsbury Park
London N4 3SR
071 272 7774

Sickle Cell Society
54 Station Road
London NW10 4UA
081 961 7795

SKILL
(National Bureau for Handicapped
   Students)
336 Brixton Road
London SW9 7AA
071 274 0565

Organisation and address	Local contact	Tel. no.

Spastics Society
12 Park Crescent
London W1N 4EQ
071 636 5020

Special Education Consortium
c/o Council for Disabled Children
8 Wakley Street
London EC1V 7QE
071 278 9441

Tuberous Sclerosis Association of GB
Martell Mount
Holywell Road
Malvern Wells
Worcs WR14 4LF
06845 63150

Young Minds
22A Boston Place
London NW1 6ER
071 724 7262

Index